GoodFood

101 BARBECUES AND GRILLS

Published in 2009 by BBC Books,
an imprint of Ebury Publishing
A Random House Group company

Recipes © BBC Magazines 2009
Book design © Woodlands Books 2009
All photographs © BBC Magazines 2009
All recipes contained within this book first
appeared in BBC *Good Food* magazine

The Random House Group Limited
Reg. No. 954009

Addresses for companies within the
Random House Group can be found at
www.randomhouse.co.uk

A CIP catalogue record for this book is available
from the British Library.

The Random House Group Limited supports
The Forest Stewardship Council (FSC), the
leading international forest certification organization.
All our titles that are printed on Greenpeace
approved FSC certified paper carry the FSC logo.
Our paper procurement policy can be found at
www.rbooks.co.uk/environment

To buy books by your favourite authors and
register for offers visit www.rbooks.co.uk

Printed and bound by Firmengruppe APPL,
aprinta druck, Wemding, Germany
Colour origination by Dot Gradations Ltd, UK

Commissioning Editor: Lorna Russell
Project Editor: Laura Higginson
Designer: Annette Peppis
Production: Lucy Harrison
Picture Researcher: Gabby Harrington

ISBN: 9781846077241

GoodFood

101 BARBECUES AND GRILLS
TRIPLE-TESTED RECIPES

Editor
Sarah Cook

BOOKS

Contents

Introduction   6

Chicken and pork   10

Beef and lamb   48

Fish and seafood   80

Vegetarian summer   116

Salads, salsas and sides   144

Al fresco drinks and desserts   178

Index   212

Introduction

Barbecuing is becoming more and more popular – it's healthy, quick and versatile, and a great excuse for getting outdoors. Also, by sticking to a few simple rules, cooking on the barbecue can be as easy or as impressive as you want it to be.

Whether you're entertaining a crowd or just rustling up a simple supper for friends or family, we've got it covered with 101 of our favourite al fresco recipes. From tasty burgers to whole marinated fish, we've also got lots of clever vegetarian ideas, and even some inspiration for salads and desserts so you can mix and match as much as you like. There really is something for everybody – take our *Falafel burgers*, pictured opposite (see page 118 for the recipe) – it's a favourite with meat-eaters and vegetarians alike.

As always, all these recipes have been triple tested by the *Good Food* team, so you can be confident you'll get great results every time. Plus, to make this little book even more useful, we've added lots of tips and instructions for cooking indoors, in case the weather lets you down at the last minute, or you simply fancy a burger in December! So all you have to do is fire up that barbecue and get grilling!

Sarah

Sarah Cook
Good Food magazine

Notes and conversion tables

NOTES ON THE RECIPES
• Eggs are large in the UK and Australia and extra large in America unless stated otherwise.
• Wash fresh produce before preparation.
• Recipes contain nutritional analyses for 'sugar', which means the total sugar content including all natural sugars in the ingredients, unless otherwise stated.

OVEN TEMPERATURES

Gas	°C	Fan °C	°F	Oven temp.
¼	110	90	225	Very cool
½	120	100	250	Very cool
1	140	120	275	Cool or slow
2	150	130	300	Cool or slow
3	160	140	325	Warm
4	180	160	350	Moderate
5	190	170	375	Moderately hot
6	200	180	400	Fairly hot
7	220	200	425	Hot
8	230	210	450	Very hot
9	240	220	475	Very hot

APPROXIMATE WEIGHT CONVERSIONS
• All the recipes in this book list both imperial and metric measurements. Conversions are approximate and have been rounded up or down. Follow one set of measurements only; do not mix the two.
• Cup measurements, which are used by cooks in Australia and America, have not been listed here as they vary from ingredient to ingredient. Kitchen scales should be used to measure dry/solid ingredients.

SPOON MEASURES

Spoon measurements are level unless otherwise specified.

• 1 teaspoon (tsp) = 5ml
• 1 tablespoon (tbsp) = 15ml
• 1 Australian tablespoon = 20ml (cooks in Australia should measure 3 teaspoons where 1 tablespoon is specified in a recipe)

APPROXIMATE LIQUID CONVERSIONS

metric	imperial	AUS	US
50ml	2fl oz	¼ cup	¼ cup
125ml	4fl oz	½ cup	½ cup
175ml	6fl oz	¾ cup	¾ cup
225ml	8fl oz	1 cup	1 cup
300ml	10fl oz/½ pint	½ pint	1¼ cups
450ml	16fl oz	2 cups	2 cups/1 pint
600ml	20fl oz/1 pint	1 pint	2½ cups
1 litre	35fl oz/1¾ pints	1¾ pints	1 quart

These delicious burgers will also cook perfectly in the oven – heat to 200°C/fan 180°C/Gas 6 and cook for about 25 minutes.

Sticky sausage burgers with blue cheese

6 pork sausages
50g/2oz fresh breadcrumbs
4 tbsp caramelized onion chutney
10 fresh sage leaves, chopped
50g/2oz blue cheese, cut into 4 chunks
4 burger buns and salad, to serve

Takes 35 minutes • Serves 4

1 Using scissors, snip open the sausage skins and squeeze the meat into a bowl, discarding the skins. Add the breadcrumbs, 2 tablespoons of the chutney, and the sage, then mix well with your hands. Divide the mix into four, then shape into burgers, pushing the chunks of cheese into the middle of each patty. Make sure the cheese is completely sealed in or it will leak out during cooking.
2 Barbecue the burgers for 10 minutes on each side until cooked through. Split open the buns, stuff each with your favourite salad and a burger, and the remaining chutney.

• Per burger 436 kcalories, protein 16g, carbohydrate 27g, fat 30g, saturated fat 11g, fibre 2g, sugar 9g, salt 2.71g

Bring a taste of the Caribbean to your barbecue with this sticky chicken dish.

Rice and peas with mango chicken

6 tbsp mango chutney
zest and juice of 2 limes
4 boneless skinless chicken breasts
2 tbsp olive oil

FOR THE RICE AND PEAS
2 tbsp olive oil
1 onion, chopped
2 garlic cloves, crushed
200g/8oz long grain rice
400g can kidney beans, drained and rinsed
400g can black eye beans, drained and rinsed
500ml/1¼ pint vegetable stock
200ml/7fl oz reduced-fat coconut milk
1 fresh thyme sprig, leaves stripped
175g/6oz frozen peas

Takes 40 minutes, plus marinating
Serves 4

1 Make the rice and peas: heat the oil in a frying pan, then fry onion for 5 minutes. Add the garlic, then stir in the rice, cooking for 1 minute more. Add the beans, pour in the stock and coconut milk, and season well. Bring to the boil, cover, then simmer gently for 25–30 minutes, until the rice is just cooked. Add the thyme leaves and peas for the final 3 minutes of cooking, then fluff up with a fork.
2 Meanwhile, mix together the mango chutney, lime zest and juice and olive oil, then season well. Heat a barbecue or a frying pan over a medium–high heat, brush a little of the mango mix over the chicken breasts, then cook for 6–8 minutes each side until charred and cooked through. Once done, set aside to rest while you heat the rest of the mango mix in the pan. Serve the chicken with the rice and peas and spoonfuls of tangy mango sauce.

• Per serving 702 kcalories, protein 50g, carbohydrate 86g, fat 20g, saturated fat 7g, fibre 11g, sugar 19g, salt 2.55g

Pork with fruit is a classic pairing – use peaches or apricots in summer and apples or pears in autumn.

Pork and peach kebabs with Little Gem salad

500g/1lb 2oz lean pork fillet, trimmed of any fat
2 peaches
1 lemon
2 tbsp clear honey
2 Little Gem lettuces
100g bag watercress
2 tbsp olive oil
1 tsp Dijon mustard

Takes 25–30 minutes • Serves 4

1 Soak 8 wooden skewers in cold water for 20–30 minutes. Cut the pork into large cubes. Halve and stone the peaches, then cut into chunks. Grate the zest from half the lemon and squeeze out the juice.

2 Reserve 1 tablespoon of the lemon juice, then mix the remainder with the zest and honey. Alternately thread the pork cubes and peach chunks onto the skewers. Brush all over with the honey and lemon mix, then barbecue for 10–12 minutes, turning regularly, until cooked.

3 Meanwhile, separate the lettuce leaves and mix with the watercress. Whisk the reserved lemon juice with the olive oil, mustard, and a little seasoning. Toss with the salad leaves and serve with the kebabs.

• Per serving (two kebabs) 257 kcalories, protein 29g, carbohydrate 11g, fat 11g, saturated fat 2g, fibre 2g, sugar 11g, salt 0.58g

Perfect if you're short of time, this simply marinated chicken is dressed up with shop-bought accompaniments.

Griddled chicken mezze

4 boneless skinless chicken breast fillets
grated zest and juice of 1 lemon
2 tbsp extra virgin olive oil, plus extra for drizzling
2 garlic cloves, crushed
¼ tsp dried thyme
houmous, kalamata olives and lemon wedges, to serve

Takes 20 minutes • Serves 4

1 Mix the chicken breasts with the lemon zest, 2 tablespoons lemon juice, the olive oil, garlic and thyme.
2 Season, then cook on a heated griddle over a medium–high heat or barbecue for 6–8 minutes each side. Serve the chicken with a generous dollop of houmous, a drizzle of olive oil, plus the olives and lemon wedges.

• Per serving 201 kcalories, protein 34g, carbohydrate 1g, fat 7g, saturated fat 1g, fibre none, added sugar none, salt 0.21g

For a lighter alternative, you could try swapping the pork for prawns – it's just as delicious.

Asian pork with rice noodle salad

1 tsp lemongrass paste
1 tsp finely grated fresh root ginger
½ red chilli, seeded and finely chopped
1 tsp sunflower oil
1 tbsp fish sauce
4 pork chops

FOR THE SALAD
200g/8oz thin rice noodles
2 tbsp fish sauce
zest and juice of 1 lime
½ tsp caster sugar
½ cucumber, seeded and sliced into thin strips
a handful of chopped fresh mint leaves

Takes 20 minutes • Serves 4

1 To make the marinade, mix together the lemongrass paste, ginger, chilli, oil and fish sauce. Smear over the pork to marinate while you make the salad.

2 Prepare the noodles according to the packet instructions. Drain, rinse under cold water to cool, then drain again and tip into a bowl. Whisk the fish sauce with the lime zest, lime juice and sugar. Pour over the cold noodles and toss together with the cucumber and mint.

3 Heat a barbecue or griddle pan over a medium–high heat and cook the chops for 5 minutes on each side or until cooked through. Serve with the noodle salad.

• Per serving 500 kcalories, protein 38g, carbohydrate 46g, fat 19g, saturated fat 7g, fibre 2g, sugar 1g, salt 2.48g

You can cook this dish straight away or, if you have time, keep it in the fridge for up to a day for the flavours to work their magic.

Zesty ginger chicken

4 boneless chicken breasts, skin on
1 tsp black peppercorns, crushed in a pestle and mortar
3cm knob of fresh root ginger, peeled and grated
2 garlic cloves, crushed
1 tbsp soy sauce
zest 1 and juice of 2 limes, plus lime wedges to serve

Takes 30 minutes • Serves 4

1 Slash each chicken breast three times and put in a shallow dish. Mix together the peppercorns, ginger, garlic, soy sauce, lime zest and juice, then pour over the chicken and leave to marinate for at least 10 minutes or up to 24 hours in the fridge.
2 Barbecue or grill on a moderate heat for 6–8 minutes on each side until cooked. Transfer to a serving dish and serve with wedges of lime for squeezing over.

• Per serving 225 kcalories, protein 37g, carbohydrate 2g, fat 8g, saturated fat 2g, fibre none, sugar 1g, salt 0.87g

Adding a splash of coconut milk to the curry-paste marinade helps to keep the chicken moist, without causing flames or smoke as oil can do. You might also like to try it with a spoonful of natural yogurt instead.

Red curry chicken kebabs

2 boneless skinless chicken breasts, cut into large chunks
2 tbsp Thai red curry paste
2 tbsp coconut milk
1 red pepper, seeded and cut into chunks
1 courgette, halved and cut into chunks
1 red onion, cut into large chunks
1 lime, cut into wedges, to garnish
herby rice and green salad, to serve

Takes 20 minutes • Serves 2 (easily doubled)

1 Fire up the barbecue or heat a griddle pan to hot. Tip the chicken, curry paste and coconut milk into a bowl, then mix well until the chicken is evenly coated.
2 Thread the vegetables and chicken chunks alternately onto four skewers, and cook on the barbecue or griddle for 5–8 minutes, turning every so often, until the chicken is cooked through and charred. Serve with lime wedges to squeeze over and some herby rice and a green salad.

• Per kebab 251 kcalories, protein 36g, carbohydrate 10g, fat 8g, saturated fat 3g, fibre 2g, sugar 8g, salt 0.85g

If it rains, cook this in exactly the same way on top of the stove – if possible, straddle the roasting tin over two rings for more even heat.

Pan-roasted chicken with crisp prosciutto and tomatoes

2 tbsp olive oil
6 slices prosciutto (about 85g/3oz)
6 boneless skinless chicken breasts, seasoned
4 garlic cloves, chopped
2 × 400g cans chopped tomatoes
150ml/¼ pint chicken or vegetable stock
4 fresh oregano sprigs, leaves removed and chopped
400g can cannellini beans, drained and rinsed
100g/4oz soft butter
1 ciabatta loaf, cut into 12 slices
250g punnet cherry tomatoes, halved
a handful of fresh basil leaves, half chopped, half left whole

Takes 50–60 minutes • Serves 6

1 Heat the oil in a sturdy roasting tin on the barbecue and crisp the prosciutto on both sides. Set aside.
2 Brown the chicken on both sides in the tin. Stir in half of the chopped garlic, the chopped tomatoes, stock and oregano. Simmer for 12 minutes, turning the chicken frequently and tipping in the beans halfway through cooking. Meanwhile, mix the remaining garlic with the butter and toast the ciabatta on the barbecue.
3 Stir the cherry tomatoes, chopped basil and some seasoning into the chicken and cook for a further 2 minutes. Top the chicken with the prosciutto and whole basil leaves, and serve with the toasted ciabatta spread with garlic bread.

• Per serving 550 kcalories, protein 54.5g, carbohydrate 32g, fat 23g, saturated fat 11g, fibre 5g, added sugar none, salt 2.59g

Toasting sandwiches on the barbecue adds a lovely smoky flavour to the bread.

Mozzarella and prosciutto panini

4 thin slices ciabatta bread, cut diagonally for longer slices
4 slices prosciutto
4 slices mozzarella, about ½ a 125g pack
1 roasted red pepper from a jar, halved
8 large fresh basil leaves
olive oil, for brushing

Takes 10 minutes • Serves 1 (easily doubled)

1 Heat a barbecue or put a griddle pan over a gentle heat to warm. Take the bread and make two sandwiches, layering up the prosciutto, mozzarella, red pepper and basil for the filling. Brush the outsides of the bread with oil.

2 Put the sandwiches on the griddle or barbecue grill and cook for about 1 minute on each side, pressing down firmly with a metal spatula so they flatten and become golden and ridged. Eat while deliciously hot and melted.

• Per serving 622 kcalories, protein 37g, carbohydrate 37g, fat 36g, saturated fat 13g, fibre 4g, added sugar none, salt 7.97g

To griddle, heat the pan to medium–hot, then cook the chicken for 20–30 minutes on each side, sprinkling with the water or beer if it gets too dry.

Spatchcock barbecue chicken

1.3kg/3lb chicken, spatchcocked
(ask your butcher to do this)
a little beer or water, to baste
2 lemons, quartered, to serve

FOR THE MARINADE
3 tbsp olive oil, plus extra to serve
1 tsp paprika, plus
extra to serve
1 garlic clove, crushed
zest and juice of 1 lemon

Takes 70–80 minutes, plus marinating
Serves 2–4

1 For the marinade, mix together the oil, paprika, garlic, lemon zest and some seasoning. Brush this all over the skin of the chicken and leave in the fridge for 30 minutes to marinate.

2 Before barbecuing, make sure the heat is moderate or the skin will burn before the chicken is cooked. Cook for around 40 minutes, turning every 5–10 minutes and basting occasionally with beer or water. To check that the chicken is cooked, pierce with a knife between the thigh and breast bone: the juices should be run clear.

3 Remove from the heat and leave to rest, covered with foil, for 10–15 minutes. Cut into portions, drizzle over the lemon juice, a little extra oil, pinches of paprika and season. Serve with the lemon quarters.

• Per serving 650 kcalories, protein 59g, carbohydrate 1g, fat 45g, saturated fat 14g, fibre 1g, added sugar none, salt 0.91g

Try using thick, woody, fresh rosemary sprigs instead of wooden skewers. They look pretty and help flavour the pork from the inside.

Pork, lemon and potato kebabs

16 baby new potatoes
700g/1lb 8oz pork tenderloin
oil, for brushing
lemon wedges, to serve

FOR THE LEMON MARINADE
2 tbsp chopped fresh rosemary
leaves, or 2 tsp dried
3 tbsp olive oil
juice of ½ lemon

Takes 35–45 minutes • Serves 4

1 Cook the potatoes in boiling salted water for 10–12 minutes until barely tender. Drain well. Trim the pork of any excess fat and cut into 3cm cubes. Thread the pork alternately with the potatoes onto eight skewers.
2 Get the barbecue going or turn the grill to a medium–high heat. Mix the chopped rosemary, olive oil and lemon juice together for the marinade and season.
3 Brush the marinade over the pork and potatoes. Barbecue or grill for 14 minutes, turning once. Brush with a little oil halfway through cooking. Serve with the lemon wedges.

• Per serving 360 kcalories, protein 39g, carbohydrate 17g, fat 16g, saturated fat 3g, fibre 1g, added sugar none, salt 0.55g

Minced turkey or pork would also work well with these fragrant and fiery flavours.

Thai-spiced chicken burgers

500g/1lb 2oz chicken mince
85g/3oz fresh breadcrumbs
2–3 tbsp red Thai curry paste
1 bunch of spring onions,
finely chopped
1 egg, beaten
1 tbsp sunflower oil
4 ciabatta rolls, mango chutney
mixed with an equal quantity of
natural yogurt, and green salad,
to serve

Takes 25 minutes, plus chilling
Makes 4 (easily doubled)

1 Put the mince, breadcrumbs, curry paste, spring onions and egg into a large bowl. Season lightly, then mix well with your hands to combine. Divide into four and shape into burgers. Chill for 20 minutes.

2 Brush the burgers with the oil and barbecue or grill on a medium–high heat for 7–10 minutes on each side or until golden and cooked through.

3 Once cooked, toast the rolls, cut-side up, on the barbecue or under the grill. Fill each roll with a chicken burger, and add some salad to serve and a spoonful of creamy mango chutney.

• Per burger 286 kcalories, protein 34g, carbohydrate 18g, fat 9g, saturated fat 1g, fibre 1g, sugar 2g, salt 1.2g

You can keep the ribs uncooked in the fridge for up to 3 days or freeze them for several months.

Sizzling spare ribs with BBQ sauce

4 × 500g packs meaty pork spare ribs
1 bunch of spring onions, roughly chopped
1 Scotch bonnet chilli, seeded and finely chopped
4 garlic cloves, roughly chopped
6 tbsp rum
6 tbsp demerara sugar
6 tbsp dark soy sauce
6 tbsp clear honey
6 tsp Dijon mustard
1 tsp ground allspice

Takes 30–35 minutes • Serves 6

1 Tip the ribs into a big bowl (not a metal one) with all the other ingredients and sprinkle with some salt and pepper. Get your hands in the bowl and turn the ribs over and over again until they are completely coated in the sauce.

2 Remove the ribs from the sauce and reserve the remaining sauce. Cook the ribs on a barbecue or under the grill on a medium–high heat for 20–30 minutes, depending on their size, turning them frequently and brushing with the remaining sauce each time. (The turning and brushing is important, so that all four sides of each rib get covered with the sauce.) If you have any extra leftover sauce at the end, heat until boiling in a pan and pour it over the ribs just before serving.

• Per serving 484 kcalories, protein 33g, carbohydrate 32g, fat 22g, saturated fat 8g, fibre none, added sugar 28g, salt 3.09g

The whole family will love this recipe – and it's easily increased to feed a bigger crowd.

Lime and pepper chicken wraps

4 boneless skinless chicken breasts, each cut into 6 strips
zest and juice of 2 limes
2 tsp black peppercorns, coarsely crushed
1 tbsp sunflower oil
8 tortilla wraps
200g tub guacamole
1 Little Gem lettuce, shredded
150ml pot low-fat natural yogurt

Takes 15 minutes • Serves 4

1 Toss the chicken with the lime zest and juice, pepper, oil and a little salt. Cook on a barbecue or griddle pan over a medium–high heat for 6–8 minutes, turning until evenly cooked and nicely browned.

2 Heat the tortillas, following the packet instructions. Spread a little guacamole over each tortilla, top with some lettuce and chicken, then drizzle over the yogurt. Roll up and enjoy.

• Per wrap 464 kcalories, protein 43g, carbohydrate 50g, fat 12g, saturated fat 2g, fibre 2g, sugar 5g, salt 2.85g

This dish is ideal for al fresco entertaining – just serve with some crusty ciabatta for mopping up juices.

Barbecued pork with sage, lemon and prosciutto

85g pack prosciutto
3 lemons
3 tbsp roughly chopped fresh sage leaves
3 × 350–450g/12oz–1lb pork tenderloins, trimmed of any fat
oil, for brushing
50g/2oz butter, chilled and cut into thin slices
sprigs of fresh sage, to garnish

Takes 40–50 minutes • Serves 8

1 In a food processor, whiz together the prosciutto, lemon zest from three lemons and juice of one and a half lemons, the chopped sage and plenty of seasoning until blended to give a thick paste. Reserve the remaining lemon halves.
2 Cut each tenderloin lengthways down the centre, but not all the way through. Open out the meat and flatten slightly. Make about 10 deep slashes in each tenderloin, cutting about three-quarters of the way through. Rub the paste over the meat and into the slashes.
3 Brush the tenderloins with oil and barbecue or grill, paste-side down, for 6–8 minutes. Turn over and cook for a further 6–8 minutes or until cooked through.
4 Transfer the pork to a serving dish. Top with the slices of butter. Leave to melt, then squeeze over the juice of the reserved lemon halves. Scatter with sage and serve.

• Per serving 255 kcalories, protein 32g, carbohydrate 1g, fat 13.6g, saturated fat 6g, fibre none, added sugars none, salt 0.62g

Corn on the cob is a great accompaniment to barbecued chicken. Brush the cobs with oil, but don't season them, as salt toughens the corn. Cook for 5–7 minutes, turning frequently, until lightly charred.

Cajun chicken

4 boneless skinless chicken breasts
1 tsp dried onion flakes
1 tbsp paprika
¼ tsp cayenne pepper
2 tsp dried thyme
1 tbsp sunflower oil
200g tub guacamole, to serve

Takes about 25 minutes • Serves 4

1 Dry the chicken with kitchen paper, then cut diagonal slashes in the surface of the smooth side. Mix the onion flakes, spices and thyme with some seasoning, then tip onto a plate.
2 Brush the chicken on both sides with the oil, then coat all over with the spice mix. Heat a barbecue, griddle pan or grill to medium–high, then cook the chicken for 5–6 minutes on each side until cooked through. Serve with a dollop of guacamole.

• Per serving 190 kcalories, protein 34g, carbohydrate 2g, fat 5g, saturated fat 1g, fibre none, sugar none, salt 0.22g

If using wooden or bamboo skewers, soak eight of them in cold water for about half an hour before you need them.

Herbed chicken skewers

500g/1lb 2oz tiny new potatoes
3 tbsp each chopped fresh parsley, mint and snipped chives
6 tbsp olive oil
2 tbsp fresh lemon juice
500g/1lb 2oz boneless skinless chicken breasts, cut into 3cm chunks
1 red onion, peeled, cut into 6 wedges, layers separated
1 red pepper, seeded and cut into 3cm chunks
1 lemon, cut into 8 wedges
1 small tub tomato salsa, to serve

Takes 40–50 minutes • Serves 8

1 Cook the potatoes in boiling salted water for 10–12 minutes until just tender. Drain and cool.
2 Mix the herbs, oil, lemon juice and seasoning in a large bowl, and add the chicken, cooled potatoes, onion and pepper, and mix thoroughly.
3 Thread the chicken and vegetables onto 8 skewers, finishing each with a lemon wedge. Barbecue or grill on a medium–high heat for 5–6 minutes on each side, until the chicken is cooked. Pile on to a serving platter with some tomato salsa on the side.

• Per skewer (not including salsa) 149 kcalories, protein 16.7g, carbohydrate 12.8g, fat 3.8g, saturated fat 0.6g, fibre 1.2g, sugar 3.1g, salt 0.12g

Driven indoors by the weather? Cook these sausages on a hot griddle pan for 15 minutes, turning often until they are cooked through.

Cumberland hot dogs with charred tomato salsa

4 Cumberland sausages
4 tomatoes, halved
1 red chilli, seeded and finely chopped
1 garlic clove, finely chopped
2 tbsp chopped fresh basil
a pinch of brown sugar
2 tbsp olive oil
1 tbsp red wine vinegar
4 hot dog rolls, salad leaves, and soured cream, to serve

Takes 25 minutes • Serves 4

1 Barbecue or griddle the sausages for 10–15 minutes, turning occasionally, until cooked through. Meanwhile, cook the tomatoes, alongside the sausages, cut-side up, for 3–4 minutes, until the skins start to blacken. Transfer to a bowl.
2 Mash the tomatoes with a fork and stir in the remaining ingredients. Spoon some into a long roll, add salad leaves, a sausage and top with a dollop of soured cream.

• Per hot dog 233 kcalories, protein 10g, carbohydrate 8g, fat 18g, saturated fat 6g, fibre 1g, sugar 5g, salt 1.28g

If you don't fancy getting the barbecue out, heat the oven to 200°C/ fan 180°C/Gas 6 and roast the drumsticks for 30 minutes until cooked through.

Spicy yogurt chicken

8 skinless chicken drumsticks
142g pot natural yogurt
1 tsp chilli powder
1 tbsp ground cumin
1 tbsp ground coriander
2 tsp ground turmeric

Takes 30 minutes • Serves 4

1 With a sharp knife, make a few slashes in each drumstick. Mix the remaining ingredients in a bowl and season. Add the drumsticks, rubbing the mixture well into the meat. If you have time, cover and chill for 30 minutes.
2 Remove the drumsticks from the marinade, shaking off the excess. Cook them on a barbecue for 20–25 minutes, turning occasionally, until cooked through.

• Per serving 229 kcalories, protein 37g, carbohydrate 6g, fat 7g, saturated fat 2g, fibre none, sugar 2g, salt 0.49g

Choose the best-quality beef mince you can get for these really easy burgers, or buy meat from the butcher and mince your own.

Classic beef burgers

500g pack lean minced beef
1 tsp mild chilli powder
4 slices cheddar (optional)
4 burger baps

FOR THE TOPPINGS
lettuce, tomatoes, cucumber,
gherkins, red onion, and
mayonnaise or ketchup, to serve

Takes 20 minutes • Serves 4

1 Put the mince in a mixing bowl with the chilli powder and some seasoning. Mix well with your hands or a fork, then divide the mixture into four and shape into burgers.
2 Fry the burgers on a hot griddle or grill them outside on the barbecue for 5 minutes on each side. For cheese burgers, put a slice of cheese on top of the burgers after you've turned them over and let it melt while the other side cooks.
3 Meanwhile, prepare the toppings of your choice. Separate lettuce leaves and slice the tomatoes, cucumber, gherkins and onion. Cut the burger baps in half and warm them in the toaster or on the barbecue. Spread a little mayonnaise or ketchup onto the buns, and fill with a burger and your favourite salad accompaniments.

• Per burger 496 kcalories, protein 39g, carbohydrate 26g, fat 27g, saturated fat 12g, fibre 1g, sugar 2g, salt 1.53g

Dressed vegetables, like these peas, make great summer side dishes, as unlike salad leaves they don't go limp so can be prepared ahead. Make and chill, then bring to room temperature just before serving.

Charred lamb with peas, mint and feta

4 lamb leg steaks
300g/10oz frozen peas
3 tbsp olive oil
grated zest and juice of 1 lemon
100g/4oz feta, crumbled
a small handful of fresh mint leaves, roughly chopped
2 spring onions, finely sliced

Takes 15 minutes • Serves 4

1 Season the lamb, then cook on a barbecue or hot griddle for 3–4 minutes on each side or until done to your liking.
2 Meanwhile, cook the peas in a large pan of boiling water for about 2 minutes until just tender. Drain, then tip the hot peas into a bowl and toss with the olive oil, lemon zest and juice. Stir through the feta, mint and spring onions, then season to taste. Serve the warm pea salad with the lamb steaks.

• Per serving 435 kcalories, protein 45g, carbohydrate 8g, fat 25g, saturated fat 10g, fibre 4g, sugar 3g, salt 1.14g

Too hot for a roast dinner? Take it outside with this stunning beef recipe. Just add potato and roasted vegetable salads to complete the menu.

Seared beef with orange and chilli

1.5kg/3lb 5oz piece skirt of beef
zest of 2 oranges
2 red chillies, seeded and finely chopped
2 shallots, finely chopped
2 tbsp olive oil
2 tbsp red wine vinegar

Takes 35 minutes, plus marinating
Serves 8

1 Wipe the beef and put in a large food bag. Mix together all the remaining ingredients, then pour over the meat in the bag. Massage the marinade into the beef, then put on a plate in the fridge for at least 2 hours, or overnight if you have time.

2 Light the barbecue, allowing time for the coals to turn grey. Season the beef with salt and pepper, then cook for 8–10 minutes on each side until well browned. Spoon over a little of the marinade as it cooks.

3 Remove the beef from the barbecue and set it on a board. Cover tightly with foil and leave to rest for 10 minutes, then cut the beef across the grain into slices.

• Per serving 360 kcalories, protein 47g, carbohydrate none, fat 19g, saturated fat 7g, fibre none, sugar none, salt 0.34g

Vary the flavour of these easy skewers by using different sauces.

Oriental beef skewers with cucumber salad

4 thin-cut sirloin steaks or minute steaks, trimmed of fat and each cut into 3 strips
120ml sachet stir-fry sauce
1 tbsp sesame seeds

FOR THE SALAD
1 tsp white wine vinegar
1 tsp light soy sauce
1 cucumber, seeded and cut into small chunks
3 spring onions, sliced
½ red chilli, seeded and finely chopped
a handful of fresh coriander leaves, chopped
steamed basmati or jasmine rice, to serve

Takes 15 minutes • Serves 4

1 Heat a barbecue or grill to High. In a bowl, mix the steak strips with the stir-fry sauce and sesame seeds. Thread the steak strips onto 12 skewers, then barbecue or grill for 6 minutes, turning halfway through, until golden and sticky.
2 Meanwhile, make the salad. Mix together the vinegar and soy sauce, then toss with the cucumber, spring onions, chilli and coriander. Serve with the beef skewers and some basmati or jasmine rice.

• Per serving 228 kcalories, protein 32g, carbohydrate 8g, fat 8g, saturated fat 3g, fibre 1g, sugar 8g, salt 2.21g

Even if you're not feeding a crowd, make the full recipe then just freeze any spare burgers, uncooked, for up to 3 months. Much tastier later than a take-away.

Kofta pitta pockets

1kg/2lb 4oz minced lamb
2 onions, coarsely grated
1 garlic bulb, broken into cloves and crushed
6 tbsp garam masala
1 bunch of fresh coriander, chopped
1 tbsp chilli sauce, plus extra to serve

TO SERVE
8 pitta breads
4 tomatoes, halved and sliced
½ red cabbage, shredded
1 red onion, sliced
1 small pot natural yogurt

Takes 35 minutes • Serves 8
(easily halved)

1 Tip the mince into a large bowl with all the other burger ingredients and some salt. Get your hands in and mix everything together thoroughly. Shape the mix into 16 small burgers, and chill until you're ready to cook.
2 Heat the barbecue or a grill until really hot, and cook the burgers for 5–6 minutes on each side until slightly charred and cooked through – you'll need to do these in batches if you're grilling. To serve, pile the burgers onto a platter with all the accompaniments, so everyone can construct their own.

• Per burger 295 kcalories, protein 26g, carbohydrate 8g, fat 18g, saturated fat 8g, fibre 1g, sugar 2g, salt 0.37g

A treat for two – perfect for a summer's evening with a glass of red wine.

Steak and roast vegetables with sun-dried tomato dressing

2 medium sweet potatoes, peeled and cut into chunks
2 red peppers, seeded and cut into chunks
2 tbsp olive oil
200g/8oz fine green beans
2 garlic cloves, thinly sliced
4 sun-dried tomatoes, finely chopped
a squeeze of lemon juice
2 sirloin steaks, about 175g/6oz each

Takes 40 minutes • Serves 2

1 Preheat the oven to 200°C/fan 180°C/Gas 6. Put the potatoes and peppers in a roasting tin, drizzle over 1 tablespoon of the oil, and roast for 20 minutes or until the edges are charred. Add the beans and garlic, stir, then cook for another 10 minutes.
2 Meanwhile, mix together the sun-dried tomatoes, lemon juice and ½ tbsp of olive oil with some pepper to make the dressing.
3 Season the steaks well, brush them with the remaining oil, and cook on a hot barbecue for a couple of minutes on each side for rare–medium – or longer if you like. Serve the steak with the roasted vegetables and a little dressing spooned over.

• Per serving 613 kcalories, protein 38.4g, carbohydrate 53.5g, fat 28.7g, saturated fat 8.8g, fibre 9.7g, sugar 21.8g, salt 1.34g

A lovely lamb dish, inspired by some favourite Greek ingredients to add some extra sunshine to a summer's day.

BBQ lamb with houmous

1 red onion, halved and thinly sliced
3 tbsp olive oil
squeeze of fresh juice juice
2 courgettes, thickly sliced
8 lamb chops
2 × 400g cans chickpeas
50g/2oz feta
a handful of fresh mint leaves, finely chopped, to serve

Takes 20 minutes • Serves 4

1 Heat a barbecue and grill to high. Tip the onion, 1 tablespoon of olive oil and lemon juice into a bowl and set aside to marinate.
2 Put the sliced courgettes on a baking sheet, toss with ½ tablespoon of oil, season, and grill for 6–8 minutes, turning, until softened. Meanwhile, season the lamb and rub with another ½ tablespoon of oil. Barbecue for 3 minutes each side, depending on size, until cooked but pink in the middle. (If it's not BBQ weather, grill the lamb with the courgettes)
3 Tip the chickpeas into a sieve. Pour over boiling water to warm them, then whiz in a food processor with the remaining oil and half the feta. Add a few spoonfuls of water to loosen, season, and serve with the lamb, courgettes and onion, sprinkled with the mint and remaining feta.

• Per serving 633 kcalories, protein 44g, carbohydrate 23g, fat 41g, saturated fat 16g, fibre 6g, sugar 3g, salt 1.38g

Flavour natural yogurt with herbs and spices, and use half as a marinade and keep the rest for drizzling over when serving.

Minty lamb kebabs

150ml pot natural yogurt
1½ tbsp mint sauce
1 tsp ground cumin
300g/10oz diced lean lamb
½ small onion, cut into large chunks
2 large pitta breads
2 large handfuls of lettuce, chopped

Takes 20 minutes • Serves 2

1 Mix the yogurt and mint sauce together, then divide the mixture in half. Stir the cumin into one half and pour over the diced lamb. Mix thoroughly to coat and season well.
2 Heat the barbecue or a grill while threading the lamb onto 4 skewers, alternating with pieces of onion. Then cook for 3–4 minutes on each side, until the lamb is cooked through and the onion beginning to brown. Warm the pittas in a toaster for 1–2 minutes and split open. Stuff the pittas with the lamb, onion and lettuce, drizzling over the remaining minty yogurt to serve.

• Per stuffed pitta 538 kcalories, protein 43g, carbohydrate 62g, fat 15g, saturated fat 7g, fibre 3g, sugar 11g, salt 1.68g

Nothing beats a good steak sandwich – and here the caramelized onion makes this one a winner.

Steak and caramelized onion sandwiches

4 minute steaks or 2 × 1cm-thick sirloin steaks
1 tbsp olive oil, plus extra for drizzling
1 small ciabatta loaf
4 tbsp caramelized onions or onion marmalade
2 handfuls of watercress

Takes 10–15 minutes • Serves 2 generously

1 Preheat the barbecue or grill to a medium–high heat. Season both sides of the steaks with salt, rub with a little oil and cook on the hottest part of the barbecue (or grill) for a couple of minutes, turning. Meanwhile, slice the ciabatta in half lengthways and toast the cut sides on the barbecue or under the grill.
2 Drizzle the hot ciabatta with a little more olive oil, spread the bottom half with the onions or onion marmalade and sit the steaks on top. Cover with the watercress and top with the other half of the ciabatta. Halve and eat straight away.

• Per sandwich 525 kcalories, protein 52g, carbohydrate 33g, fat 21g, saturated fat 5g, fibre 2g, added sugar 2g, salt 1.85g

If you make double the aubergines, you can stuff it into pitta breads with houmous for lunch the next day.

Lamb chops with smoky aubergine salad

1 aubergine, thinly sliced lengthways
3 tbsp olive oil
4 lamb cutlets or chops, trimmed of fat
a squeeze of fresh lemon juice
a pinch of paprika
2 tsp chopped fresh dill
1 tbsp toasted pine nuts
salad and pitta bread, to serve

Takes 20 minutes • Serves 2

1 Heat a barbecue or a griddle pan over a high heat. Brush the aubergine slices with the oil. Season and barbecue or griddle until browned on both sides and softened. Remove from heat, then tear or chop into small pieces.

2 Griddle or barbecue the chops for 4 minutes on each side for pink.

3 To make the dressing, combine the lemon juice, paprika, half the dill and some seasoning in a bowl. Drizzle the dressing over the aubergines and toss.

4 Divide between 2 plates, top with the chops, then scatter with pine nuts and the rest of the dill. Serve with salad and pitta bread.

• Per serving 424 kcalories, protein 27g, carbohydrate 4g, fat 33g, saturated fat 9g, fibre 4g, sugar 4g, salt 0.19g

Barbecuing lean lamb leg steaks gives them a smoky flavour that tastes great with the sweet beetroot salad.

Sizzled lamb steaks with warm beetroot salad

4 lamb leg steaks, about
140g/5oz each
4 tbsp olive oil
1 large red onion, finely sliced
250g pack cooked beetroot, drained
and chopped into small chunks
410g can chickpeas, drained
and rinsed
50g/2oz rocket or watercress
a handful of fresh mint or coriander
leaves, roughly chopped

Takes 20 minutes • Serves 4

1 Put the lamb steaks in a shallow dish and add 2 tablespoons of the olive oil. Season with freshly ground black pepper and turn so they are coated with the oil.

2 Heat the rest of the oil in a shallow pan and gently fry the onion for about 5 minutes until softened. Add the chunks of beetroot and stir them around in the pan, then turn the heat to very low and tip in the chickpeas – don't stir. Keep them warm while you cook the lamb.

3 Heat your barbecue or a heavy-based frying pan. Add the lamb steaks and cook them over a fairly fierce heat for about 3 minutes per side for medium, or until cooked to your liking.

4 Divide the salad leaves among the 4 plates, top with the warm beetroot salad and scatter with half the mint or coriander. Top with the lamb, sliced, and scatter with remaining herbs.

• Per serving 371 kcalories, protein 32g, carbohydrate 17g, fat 20g, saturated fat 7g, fibre 4g, added sugar none, salt 0.68g

Adding healthy beetroot to burgers is a favourite in New Zealand and Australia.

Open burgers with beetroot

500g/1lb 2oz lean minced beef
100g/4oz cooked beetroot, not in vinegar
2 mini garlic and coriander naan breads
50g bag rocket
4 tbsp soured cream
green salad and chips, to serve

Takes 25 minutes • Serves 4 (easily doubled)

1 Tip the mince into a bowl and sprinkle over 1 teaspoon of salt and a good grinding of freshly ground black pepper. Work with wet hands to mix in the seasoning and then shape into 4 burgers. Slice the beetroot and halve the naan breads.

2 Heat a griddle pan or barbecue. Cook the naans on both sides until lightly toasted then set aside. Add the burgers to the grill or barbecue and cook a few minutes on each side or until done to your liking.

3 Put half a toasted naan on each serving plate and top with some rocket and a burger. Add a dollop of soured cream and serve immediately with a big green salad and chips.

• Per burger 352 kcalories, protein 33.7g, carbohydrate 30g, fat 11.4g, saturated fat 5.3g, fibre 1.9g, added sugar 0.6g, salt 1.25g

Simply barbecued steak can be transformed with a tasty rub or marinade.

Porcini-rubbed steak

25g/1oz dried porcini mushrooms
1 fresh thyme sprig, leaves only
2 thick sirloin steaks
1 tbsp olive oil
baked potatoes and salad, to serve

Takes 20 minutes, plus overnight marinating • Serves 2 (easily doubled)

1 Whiz the mushrooms into a fine powder in a small food processor or coffee grinder. Mix with a good pinch of salt, pepper and the thyme leaves. Rub the mixture all over the steaks, then pop on to a plate or into a sealable kitchen bag and chill overnight.
2 To cook, brush away any excess mixture and heat the barbecue or a griddle pan until smoking hot. Smear a little olive oil over each steak and barbecue or griddle for 3 minutes, then turn and cook for a further 2 minutes for medium–rare. Serve each steak with a baked potato and some salad.

• Per serving 428 kcalories, protein 47g, carbohydrate 1g, fat 26g, saturated fat 10g, fibre 2g, sugar none, salt 0.29g

This quick and easy salsa is also great with tuna, grilled halloumi strips or to top a home-made beef burger.

Sizzling lamb with Mexican salsa

250g/9oz ripe vine tomatoes
1 small red onion, finely chopped
1 red chilli, seeded and finely chopped
2 tbsp chopped fresh coriander
4 lamb leg steaks
a little olive oil, for cooking
new potatoes and a crunchy salad, to serve

Takes 20 minutes • Serves 4

1 Halve the tomatoes, squeeze out and discard the seeds – this seems a bit wasteful, but it really intensifies the flavour of the salsa – and chop. Mix the tomato, onion and chilli in a bowl with the coriander and some salt and pepper. If you're making it ahead, chill, then bring back to room temperature before serving.

2 Season the lamb steaks on both sides and rub with a little olive oil. Barbecue or cook on a hot griddle for 3–4 minutes each side for medium, or a little longer if you prefer your lamb well done. Serve each leg steak with a dollop of the salsa, new potatoes and a big crunchy salad.

• Per serving 306 kcalories, protein 36g, carbohydrate 3g, fat 17g, saturated fat 8g, fibre 1g, added sugar none, salt 0.24g

These tasty home-made burgers use lean mince lightened with couscous, so they're much lower in fat than most beef burgers.

Herby beef and couscous burgers

50g/2oz couscous
500g/1lb 2oz lean minced beef
1 small onion, finely chopped
2 tsp dried mixed herbs
3 tbsp snipped fresh chives
¼ tsp hot chilli powder
6 slices French bread
6 tsp Dijon mustard
175g/6oz roasted red peppers from a jar, cut into large pieces
a couple of handfuls of rocket

Takes 25–35 minutes • Serves 6

1 Tip the couscous into a bowl, pour over 5ml of boiling water and leave for a few minutes to absorb the liquid. Then stir in the mince, onion, mixed herbs, chives, chilli powder and some seasoning. Shape into 6 oval burgers, cover and chill until ready to cook.
2 Heat the barbecue or grill under a medium–high heat, then cook the burgers for 5–6 minutes on each side, or more if you like them well cooked.
3 Grill or lightly toast the slices of bread and spread with mustard. Top each slice of toast with some of the peppers and a little rocket, add a burger, and serve.

• Per burger 260 kcalories, protein 23g, carbohydrate 30g, fat 6g, saturated fat 2g, fibre 2g, added sugar none, salt 1.1g

Don't compromise on the cut of meat in these skewers, leg of lamb will really give a fantastic flavour.

Lamb skewers

8 long sprigs of rosemary, or 12–16 shorter ones
3 garlic cloves, chopped
3 tbsp extra virgin olive oil, plus extra for drizzling
20 pancetta slices, halved
40 fresh sage leaves
1 large leg of lamb (about 2.25kg/5lb), boned, trimmed of fat and cut into 3cm cubes

TO SERVE
8 thick slices of bread
1 garlic clove, peeled
lemon wedges

Takes 30-40 minutes, plus marinating
Serves 8

1 Strip the rosemary leaves from the sprigs, leaving a few on each tip. Make a paste with the leaves, garlic, olive oil and a little seasoning in a mortar and pestle.
2 Thread 1 piece of folded pancetta onto each stripped rosemary stick, followed by 1 sage leaf and 1 piece of lamb. Repeat four times and end with another piece of pancetta and a sage leaf. Spread the paste over the skewers and marinate for at least 30 minutes.
3 Grill the lamb over a medium heat on the barbecue or a large griddle pan for 10–15 minutes for medium/rare meat. Toast the bread for the last few minutes, then rub both sides with the whole garlic clove and drizzle with a little olive oil. Squeeze lemon juice over the lamb just before serving.

• Per kebab (large) 407 kcalories, protein 49g, carbohydrate 1g, fat 30g, saturated fat 12g, fibre none, sugar none, salt 1.87g

If the weather isn't great, simply make this on the hob. You might need to have two burners going if you're using a large pan or baking sheet.

Sardines with chickpeas, lemon and parsley

10 sardines, scaled and cleaned (8 if large)
50g/2oz plain flour, seasoned
zest of 2 lemons
1 large bunch flat-leaf parsley, leaves only, roughly chopped
3 garlic cloves, finely chopped
3 tbsp olive oil
1 small glass white wine
2 × 400g cans chickpeas or butter beans, drained and rinsed
250g pack cherry tomatoes, halved
crusty bread, to serve

Takes 20 minutes • Serves 6

1 Dust the sardines in the seasoned flour. Mix together the lemon zest, parsley and half of the chopped garlic, and set aside.
2 Heat the oil in a large pan (a paella pan or sturdy baking sheet) on top of the barbecue or hob until hot. Add the sardines in one layer and fry for 6 minutes, turning halfway, until golden. Lift out on to a plate.
3 Fry the remaining garlic for 1 minute until softened. Pour in the wine, scrape any bits off the bottom of the pan with a wooden spoon, and boil for 1 minute or until reduced by half.
4 Stir in the chickpeas or butter beans and tomatoes until heated through. Season, return the fish to the pan, sprinkle with the parsley mix and serve with plenty of crusty bread to mop up the juices.

• Per serving 330 kcalories, protein 24g, carbohydrate 22g, fat 16g, saturated fat 2g, fibre 4g, sugar 3g, salt 0.72g

Try this for a light supper or lunch, indoors or out.

Spiced mackerel toasts

250g pack beetroot (not in vinegar),
diced
1 eating apple, wedged then
thinly sliced
1 small red onion, finely sliced
juice of ½ lemon
1 tbsp olive oil, plus extra
for drizzling
1 tsp cumin seeds
1 small bunch of fresh coriander,
leaves roughly chopped
4 slices from a sourdough
or ciabatta loaf

FOR THE FISH
1 tsp mild curry powder
4 mackerel fillets, halved widthways
olive oil, for drizzling

Takes 15 minutes • Serves 4

1 Mix together the beetroot, apple, onion, lemon juice, oil, cumin and coriander for the salsa, season well, then set aside.
2 Heat a barbecue or grill to High. Rub the curry powder and some seasoning into the fish with a drizzle of oil. Barbecue skin-side down, or grill skin-side up, for 4–5 minutes until the skin is crisp and fillets cooked through – you won't need to turn.
3 Toast the bread, then drizzle with a little olive oil. Top with the salsa and mackerel and eat straight away.

• Per serving 471 kcalories, protein 25g, carbohydrate 35g, fat 27g, saturated fat 5g, fibre 3g, sugar 11g, salt 0.97g

Tuna is a good source of omega-3 and tastes fantastic with these sweet and spicy vegetables.

Tuna with peppery tomatoes and potatoes

4 tuna steaks
1 tbsp olive oil
3 garlic cloves, crushed
a few fresh thyme sprigs
500g bag new potatoes, sliced about 1cm thick
2 red peppers, seeded and cut into large chunks
1 red onion, cut into 8 wedges
1 green chilli, seeded and chopped
400g can cherry tomatoes

Takes 35 minutes • Serves 4

1 Put a roasting tin in the oven and preheat the oven to 220°C/fan 200°C/Gas 7. Put the tuna in a dish with half the oil, two-thirds of the garlic and leaves from 1 thyme sprig. Leave to marinate while you cook the veg.
2 Put the potatoes, peppers, onion and chilli into the roasting tin with the remaining oil, toss to coat, then roast for 20 minutes until the potatoes are almost tender. Add the remaining garlic and the thyme sprigs, let them sizzle, then stir in the tomatoes and cook for 5 minutes more until the sauce has reduced a little. Season to taste.
3 Wipe most of the garlic marinade off the fish with kitchen paper, season, then sear on the barbecue or griddle pan for 1 minute each side for medium, or longer if you prefer. Serve on top of the veg.

• Per serving 371 kcalories, protein 40g, carbohydrate 31g, fat 11g, saturated fat 2g, fibre 4g, sugar 11g, salt 0.48g

Serve this Indian-spiced fish with a leafy salad, some boiled rice and a dollop of mango chutney or cooling raita on the side.

Tikka-style fish

2 whole sea bream or red snapper, about 900g/2lb each (or use 6 meaty fish steaks, such as tuna)
2 tbsp finely grated fresh root ginger
4 garlic cloves, crushed
6 tbsp natural yogurt
2 tbsp olive oil
2 tsp turmeric
2 tsp mild chilli powder
3 tsp cumin seeds
leafy salad, plain boiled rice and mango chutney or raita, to serve

Takes 25 minutes • Serves 6

1 Slash the skin of the whole fish, if using, on each side with a sharp knife. Mix together the ginger and garlic, season with salt, then rub all over the fish (or fish steaks).
2 Mix the yogurt with the oil, spices and some seasoning. Use to coat the fish inside and out, then chill until ready to cook.
3 Heat the barbecue or grill to Medium then cook straight on the rack (or on foil if you are afraid of it sticking) for 6–8 minutes each side for the whole fish, or 3–4 minutes for the fish steaks. Serve with salad, rice and chutney or raita.

• Per serving 266 kcalories, protein 39g, carbohydrate 4g, fat 11g, saturated fat 2g, fibre none, sugar 1g, salt 0.67g

Low in fat, this salsa also works well with tuna or prawns, or even barbecued pork ribs.

Seared swordfish with mango salsa

1 tbsp olive oil
2 swordfish steaks, about 100g/4oz
each (buy from sustainable stocks)
salad leaves, to serve

FOR THE MANGO SALSA
½ ripe mango, peeled and chopped
2 spring onions, thinly sliced
1 red chilli, seeded and
finely chopped
zest and juice of ½ lime
a handful of coriander,
leaves chopped

Takes 15 minutes • Serves 2
(easily doubled)

1 Rub the oil all over the fish and season. Heat the barbecue or a griddle pan over a medium–high heat, cook the fish for 3 minutes, then turn and cook for 3 minutes on the other side until charred and just cooked through.
2 For the salsa, toss together the mango, spring onions, chilli, lime zest and juice and coriander. Serve with the grilled fish and salad leaves.

• Per serving 208 kcalories, protein 19g, carbohydrate 12g, fat 10g, saturated fat 2g, fibre 2g, sugar 12g, salt 0.34g

Cooking prawns in their shells makes all the difference to their flavour, but shelling them is messy – so provide finger bowls, too.

Piri-piri prawns

4 tbsp sunflower oil
4 garlic cloves, crushed
2 red chillies, seeded and finely chopped
¼ tsp salt
½ tsp paprika
18 large raw prawns in their shells
mint chutney or sauce, and lime slices, to serve

Takes 15 minutes • Serves 6 as a starter

1 Mix the oil with the garlic, chillies, salt and paprika, then toss in the prawns. Marinate the prawns in the fridge for up to 1 day.
2 Heat the barbecue or grill to medium–high. Cook the prawns singly or thread 3 onto 6 skewers to make portions. Cook for just a few minutes each side until they turn from grey to pink. Serve with mint chutney or sauce, finger bowls of warm water with lime slices, napkins, and a bowl for the shells.

• Per serving 134 kcalories, protein 15g, carbohydrate 1g, fat 8g, saturated fat 1g, fibre none, sugar none, salt 0.63g

Double the recipe and use leftover salmon to stuff wholemeal pittas for lunch. Add shredded lettuce, beansprouts and a little more chilli.

Thai salmon kebabs with sweet chilli and lime dip

4 tbsp sweet chilli sauce
juice of 1 lime
4 × 140g/5oz skinless salmon fillets,
cut into large chunks
oil, for drizzling

Takes 30 minutes • Serves 4

1 Combine the sweet chilli sauce and lime juice in a bowl. Pour half the mixture into a serving bowl and set aside. Thread the salmon onto 4 skewers and brush with the remaining chilli and lime sauce. Marinate for 20 minutes.
2 Heat the barbecue or a griddle pan until very hot. Shake excess marinade from the kebabs, then drizzle with oil, season and cook for 8 minutes, turning occasionally, until the salmon is opaque and flakes easily. Serve hot with the chilli and lime dipping sauce.

• Per serving 291 kcalories, protein 29g, carbohydrate 3g, fat 19g, saturated fat 4g, fibre 1g, added sugar 2g, salt 1.16g

Allowing the heat on the barbecue to die down means the skin shouldn't burn and blister before the fish is cooked through.

Barbecued mackerel with ginger, chilli and lime drizzle

4 small whole mackerel, gutted and cleaned
1 tbsp extra virgin olive oil, for brushing

FOR THE DRIZZLE
2 tbsp extra virgin olive oil
1 large red chilli, seeded and finely chopped
1 small garlic clove, finely chopped
a small knob of fresh root ginger, peeled and finely chopped
2 tsp clear honey
finely grated zest and juice of 2 large limes
1 tsp sesame oil
1 tsp Thai fish sauce
a small handful of fresh coriander leaves, chopped

Takes 25 minutes • Serves 4

1 Make the drizzle by whisking the 2 tablespoons of olive oil and all the other ingredients together, adjusting the ratio of honey to lime to make a sharp sweetness. Season.
2 Score each side of the mackerel about six times, not quite through to the bone. Brush the fish with the 1 tablespoon of oil and season lightly. Barbecue the mackerel, or grill on a medium–high heat, for 5–6 minutes on each side until the fish is charred and the eyes have turned white. Spoon the drizzle over the fish and allow to stand for 2–3 minutes before serving.

• Per serving 406 kcalories, protein 29g, carbohydrate 3g, fat 31g, saturated fat 6g, fibre none, sugar 2g, salt 0.49g

Cook the squid with the chorizo if you want to make this on the hob.

Squid, chickpea and chorizo salad

4 red peppers
2 × 400g cans chickpeas, rinsed and drained
1 huge bunch of parsley, roughly chopped
1 red chilli, seeded and chopped
2 garlic cloves, finely chopped
600g/1lb 5oz cleaned squid
100ml/3½fl oz olive oil
200g/8oz chorizo, cut into chickpea-sized chunks
juice and zest of 1 large lemon

Takes 1 hour • Serves 6–8 with other dishes

1 Cook the whole peppers under a grill or on a barbecue until completely charred. Place in a bowl, cover with a plate until cool enough to handle, then peel, seed and finely slice. Mix the peppers and any juices with the chickpeas, parsley, chilli and garlic.
2 Light the barbecue. Pat dry the squid, drizzle with a little oil and barbecue for a couple of minutes each side until just cooked. Meanwhile, stir fry the chorizo for 2 minutes in a hot pan.
3 Slice the hot squid into rings and mix into the peppers with the chorizo. Season, then dress with the remaining oil, lemon juice and lemon zest. Mix together, pile onto a platter and let everyone help themselves.

• Per serving (for six people) 443 kcalories, protein 29g, carbohydrate 22g, fat 27g, saturated fat 5g, fibre 5g, sugar 8g, salt 1.23g

All these wraps need on the side are some paprika-scented potato wedges – perfect for a relaxed dinner with friends.

Spiced tuna tortillas

1 tbsp sunflower oil
2 large tuna steaks
a pinch of cayenne pepper
1 tsp ground cumin
4 soft tortillas
1 avocado, sliced
2 tomatoes, sliced
juice of 1 lime
a handful of fresh coriander, leaves chopped
soured cream, to serve

Takes 15 minutes • Serves 4

1 Rub the oil over each steak, then sprinkle with the spices. Barbecue or griddle the steaks over a medium–high heat on one side for 2 minutes, then turn and cook for 1–2 minutes more. Cut into strips.
2 Heat the tortillas following the packet instructions. Pile the tuna, avocado and tomatoes on top of each, then squeeze over the lime juice and scatter with coriander. Dollop soured cream on top, if you like, then roll up and eat.

• Per tortilla 370 kcalories, protein 27g, carbohydrate 36g, fat 15g, saturated fat 2g, fibre 3g, sugar 2g, salt 0.54g

The courgettes and salmon strips can be cooked on a hot griddle pan if you don't fancy getting the barbecue out.

Warm salad of chargrilled courgettes and salmon

4 tbsp olive oil
juice of 1 lemon
2 tsp dried *herbes de Provence*
1 garlic clove, crushed
8 baby courgettes, each cut in half lengthways
2 skinless salmon fillets, each cut into 3 strips
85g bag herb salad, to serve

FOR THE DRESSING
3 tbsp olive oil
1 tbsp fresh lemon juice
1 tsp grainy mustard
2 tbsp chopped fresh tarragon

Takes 20–30 minutes • Serves 2
(easily doubled)

1 Make the dressing. Measure the ingredients into a jug or screw-topped jar, season, then whisk or shake to mix.
2 Now mix the olive oil, lemon juice, herbs, garlic and some seasoning in a bowl. Toss the courgettes in this marinade until coated. Shake off any excess marinade and barbecue the courgettes in batches for 2–3 minutes on each side until just softened, with stripes. Set aside. Put the salmon strips into the remaining marinade and toss to coat, then barbecue for 1–2 minutes on each side until just cooked through.
3 To serve, divide the salad leaves between two plates and lay the courgettes and salmon on top. Re-whisk the dressing and drizzle over.

• Per serving 635 kcalories, protein 31g, carbohydrate 5g, fat 55g, saturated fat 9g, fibre 1g, added sugar none, salt 0.27g

This is a clever way to cook fish on the barbecue so it doesn't dry out. To cook in the oven, heat to 180°C/fan 160°C/Gas 4 and bake for 20–25 minutes.

Lemony fish parcels

1 lemon
100g/4oz couscous
25g/1oz pine nuts, toasted
1 small courgette, thinly sliced
a small handful of fresh dill, leaves only, chopped
150ml/¼ pint strong vegetable stock
1 haddock or other firm white fish fillet

Takes 30 minutes • Serves 1 (easily doubled)

1 Fold a large sheet of foil in half and scrunch one open edge to seal (you should now have a square bag with two sealed edges and two open). Zest the lemon and mix with couscous, pine nuts, courgette and dill. Season well, then tip into the open 'bag'. Halve the lemon, then cut two thin slices from one half. Juice the other half and add to the stock.

2 Lay the fish on top of the couscous, top with lemon slices, and pour over the lemony stock. Scrunch the remaining open sides tightly to seal. Cook the parcel on the barbecue, and pull down the lid or cover with an upturned roasting tin, for 20 minutes until the fish is cooked and couscous is fluffy.

• Per serving 552 kcalories, protein 41g, carbohydrate 57g, fat 20g, saturated fat 2g, fibre 2g, sugar 6g, salt 0.46g

Seasoning the fish with coarse rock salt stops it from sticking to the barbecue or griddle.

Sardines with Sicilian fennel salad

zest and juice of 1 lemon
1 bunch of parsley, half leaves kept whole, half finely chopped
1 small garlic clove, finely chopped
1 fennel bulb, with fronds
50g/2oz toasted pine nuts
50g/2oz raisins
a handful of pitted green olives, chopped
3 tbsp olive oil, plus extra for drizzling
4 large sardines, scaled and gutted
rock salt, to season

Takes 30 minutes • Serves 2

1 Mix together the lemon zest, chopped parsley and garlic, then set aside. Pick the fronds from the fennel and set aside. Halve the fennel bulb and finely slice. Make the salad by mixing the sliced fennel and fronds with the pine nuts, raisins, olives and the whole parsley leaves. Dress with the olive oil and lemon juice.
2 Heat the barbecue or griddle pan over a medium heat. Season the sardines with rock salt. Cook for 2–3 minutes on each side until the eyes turn white. Sprinkle the fish with the lemon and parsley mix and lift on to plates. Drizzle with a little extra oil and serve with the fennel salad.

• Per serving 663 kcalories, protein 34g, carbohydrate 20g, fat 50g, saturated fat 7g, fibre 3g, sugar 20g, salt 1.49g

Fish burgers can be more delicate than meat for summer eating, and popping them in the freezer briefly before cooking should stop them falling apart.

Tangy tuna burgers

200g/8oz fresh tuna steaks
1 garlic clove, finely chopped
a small knob of fresh root ginger,
peeled and finely chopped
1 tbsp soy sauce
a handful of fresh coriander
leaves, chopped
1 tbsp sunflower oil
2 burger buns
lettuce leaves, sliced tomato and
avocado, to serve

Takes 25 minutes • Serves 2

1 Chop the tuna into small chunks, then carry on chopping until the tuna is roughly minced. Tip the tuna into a bowl and mix with the garlic, ginger, soy sauce and coriander. Shape into 2 burgers, place on a plate, then freeze for 10 minutes to firm up, or chill for a few hours.
2 Brush the burgers with the oil, then cook them for 1–2 minutes on each side, or until done to your liking, on a barbecue or in a frying pan over a medium heat. Serve the burgers in toasted buns with lettuce, tomato and avocado.

• Per burger 97 kcalories, protein 12g, carbohydrate 1g, fat 5g, saturated fat 1g, fibre none, sugar none, salt 0.74g

If using wooden or bamboo skewers, soak eight in cold water for about half an hour before threading on the prawns.

Bay-scented prawns with basil mayonnaise

2 × 20g packs fresh basil leaves
6 tbsp olive oil
250ml jar mayonnaise
juice of 1 lime
32 large raw prawns, heads and shells removed
24 small fresh bay leaves
6 tbsp olive oil

Takes 20–30 minutes • Serves 8

1 For the basil mayonnaise, put the basil leaves into a small food processor with 2 tablespoons of the olive oil. Whiz for 1–2 minutes until you have a fine paste. Add all of the mayonnaise and a squeeze of lime juice – reserving the squeezed lime halves. Blend until smooth, then transfer to a bowl and chill.

2 Thread 4 prawns and 3 bay leaves onto each skewer – you'll need 8 skewers. Brush all over with the remaining oil. Season well. Barbecue or grill on a medium–high heat for 4–5 minutes, turning once, until pink and tender. Spoon the basil mayo into the squeezed-out lime halves and serve.

• Per serving 301 kcalories, protein 11g, carbohydrate 1g, fat 28g, saturated fat 4g, fibre none, added sugar none, salt 0.65g

If your barbecue is out of action, or the weather is against you, heat the oven to 200°C/fan 180°C/Gas 6 and bake these parcels for 25 minutes.

Baked sea bass with lemongrass and ginger

1 whole sea bass, about 1.4kg/3lb, gutted and cleaned
2 tbsp olive oil, plus extra for oiling foil
3 lemongrass stalks, cut diagonally into 2.5cm pieces
2 small chillies, seeded and halved
2 garlic cloves, halved
3cm knob of fresh root ginger, peeled and cut into thin strips
1 tsp clear honey
2 limes
2 kaffir lime leaves or a few strips of lime peel

Takes 30–35 minutes • Serves 4

1 Wash the fish inside and out, patting dry with kitchen paper. Score the skin a few times on each side. Lay the fish on a large piece of oiled foil, big enough to wrap it loosely. Put the lemongrass, chillies, garlic, ginger, honey, one tablespoon of oil and the juice of the lime into a mortar and bash until everything is bruised.
2 Season the fish inside and out, and rub with half of the lemongrass mixture and the remaining oil. Cut the second lime into quarters and push two into the cavity with the remaining lemongrass mixture and the lime leaves or peel. Squeeze the juice from the last two lime quarters over the fish then crimp the edges of the foil together to create a loose parcel.
3 Place on the barbecue (away from the fiercest flames) and pull down the lid, or cover with an upturned roasting tin. Cook for 25 minutes then rest for 5 minutes before opening the parcel.

• Per serving 291 kcalories, protein 43.6g, carbohydrate 2.4g, fat 11.9g, saturated fat 1.9g, fibre 0.1g, sugar 1.3g, salt 0.40g

Barbecued or grilled fish and this fresh-tasting salsa are a perfect partnership.

Grilled fish with chunky avocado salsa

1 ripe avocado
2 ripe plum tomatoes, chopped into chunks
1 small red onion, finely sliced
3 tbsp olive oil, plus extra for drizzling
juice of ½ lemon or 1 lime
1 small bunch of fresh coriander, leaves only
2 × 140g/5oz fish fillets, such as Pacific cod or halibut, skin on

Takes 10–15 minutes • Serves 2

1 Halve and stone the avocado and use a teaspoon to scoop chunks of the flesh into a bowl. Gently mix in all the other ingredients (except the fish) with the avocado, then set aside.
2 Heat a barbecue or a griddle pan until very hot. Season the fish then drizzle with a little extra olive oil. Cook the fillets for 2–3 minutes on each side until charred and cooked through. Serve with the avocado salsa.

• Per serving 423 kcalories, protein 28g, carbohydrate 6g, fat 32g, saturated fat 4g, fibre 3g, added sugar none, salt 0.25g

A sharp, citrus-flavoured salad really brings out the best in this deliciously oily fish.

Seared tuna with parsley salad

2 line-caught yellowfin tuna steaks
1 tbsp olive oil
2 lemon wedges and some new potatoes, to serve

FOR THE SALAD
2 handfuls of flat-leaf parsley leaves, very roughly chopped
2 shallots, finely sliced
1 tbsp capers, roughly chopped
a small handful of green olives, stoned and roughly chopped
6 tbsp olive oil
1 tbsp Dijon mustard
juice of ½ lemon

Takes 20 minutes • Serves 2

1 First make the salad by mixing all the ingredients together until combined. Set aside while you cook the tuna.
2 Heat a griddle pan or barbecue until practically smoking. Rub the tuna with the olive oil and season. Cook the tuna steaks for 1 minute on each side, turning 90 degrees halfway through if you want a criss-cross pattern. If you prefer your tuna well cooked, give it a few more minutes on each side.
3 Serve each steak with half the salad, a lemon wedge for squeezing over and a few new potatoes, if you like.

• Per serving 578 kcalories, protein 35g, carbohydrate 3g, fat 48g, saturated fat 7g, fibre 2g, sugar 2g, salt 2.30g

Halloumi is a salty Greek cheese, perfect for using on the barbecue as, unlike most cheeses, it doesn't melt. It's also great for grilling when it's not barbecue weather.

Halloumi, watermelon and mint salad

250g pack halloumi, thinly sliced
flesh from 1kg/2lb 4oz chunk watermelon, sliced
200g pack fine green beans
1 small bunch of fresh mint, finely shredded
juice of 1 lemon
1 tbsp olive oil, plus extra to drizzle
toasted pitta breads, to serve

Takes 15 minutes • Serves 4

1 Barbecue or grill the halloumi on a high heat for a few minutes on each side until golden and crisp.
2 Meanwhile, toss the watermelon, beans and mint together with the lemon juice and olive oil, season well, then layer on plates with the slices of halloumi. Drizzle with a little more oil if you like, and then serve with warm pittas.

• Per serving 287 kcalories, protein 14g, carbohydrate 12g, fat 20g, saturated fat 10g, fibre 1g, sugar 12g, salt 2.29g

Harissa is a spicy paste, commonly used in Moroccan cooking – if you can't get hold of any, just use a little chilli powder in its place.

Falafel burgers

400g can chickpeas, drained and rinsed
1 small red onion, roughly chopped
1 garlic clove, chopped
a handful of fresh flat-leaf or curly parsley leaves
1 tsp each ground cumin and coriander
½ tsp harissa paste
2 tbsp plain flour
2 tbsp sunflower oil
toasted pittas, 200g tub tomato salsa and green salad, to serve

Takes 15 minutes • Serves 4

1 Pat the chickpeas dry with kitchen paper, then tip them into a food processor along with the onion, garlic, parsley, spices, harissa, flour and a little salt. Blend until fairly smooth, then shape into 4 patties with your hands.
2 Brush the burgers with the oil and then barbecue for a few minutes on each side until heated through (or heat the oil in a non-stick frying pan, add the burgers, then quickly fry for 3 minutes on each side until lightly golden). Serve with toasted pittas, tomato salsa and a green salad.

• Per burger 161 kcalories, protein 6g, carbohydrate 18g, fat 8g, saturated fat 1g, fibre 3g, sugar 1g, salt 0.36g

Adding bread to a kebab is a little unusual, but it creates a lovely crunch, especially the soft, smooth cheese.

Toasty feta kebabs

1 lemon, zested and halved lengthways
½ French stick, cut into bite-sized pieces
200g pack reduced-fat feta cheese, cut into 8 chunks
8 cherry tomatoes
2 fresh rosemary sprigs, chopped
1 tbsp olive oil

Takes 15 minutes • Serves 2

1 Cut 1 lemon half into wedges, and slice the other half. Thread a piece of the bread onto a skewer, then a chunk of feta, a lemon slice and a cherry tomato. Repeat, then finish with a piece of bread. Do this on 3 more skewers and then put the kebabs on a baking sheet.
2 Sprinkle over the lemon zest and rosemary, then drizzle over the oil. Grill on the baking sheet, under a medium–high heat or lift the kebabs on to the barbecue and cook for 1–2 minutes on each side until feta is browned. Serve with the lemon wedges.

• Per serving 732 kcalories, protein 26g, carbohydrate 61g, fat 45g, saturated fat 16g, fibre 3g, sugar 8g, salt 5.25g

If you can't find Arab flatbreads, tortillas or pitta breads are equally delicious.

Roasted pepper and halloumi wraps

2 thick slices halloumi cheese
½ tsp dried oregano
1 tbsp olive oil
2 Arab flat breads (they look like circular pitta bread)
2 roasted red peppers from a jar
6 slices roasted aubergine from a jar
a handful of Kalamata olives
4 lemon wedges
a good handful of parsley sprigs

Takes 15 minutes • Serves 2

1 Sprinkle both sides of the halloumi with the oregano, and brush with a little of the oil. Barbecue or griddle the halloumi over a medium–high heat for a few minutes each side until golden and crisp. Meanwhile, warm the flat breads over the barbecue for a few seconds (or according to packet instructions).
2 Halve the peppers (removing any stray seeds) and thickly slice, then mix with the aubergines and olives in a roasting tin. Place the tin on the barbecue or in the oven on a medium heat to warm the vegetables for a couple of minutes. Squeeze over two of the lemon wedges and season well. To serve, divide the vegetables, halloumi slices and parsley sprigs between the flat bread pockets, and top each with a lemon wedge for squeezing over.

• Per serving 561 kcalories, protein 14g, carbohydrate 51g, fat 35g, saturated fat 8g, fibre 5g, added sugar none, salt 0.91g

These versatile sauces go well with other grilled vegetables, such as courgettes and red or yellow peppers, and spicy chicken.

Aubergine with yogurt and tomato sauces

1 large fat aubergine
3 tbsp olive oil
140g/5oz cherry tomatoes, halved
1 garlic clove, crushed
a pinch of chilli flakes
small pot of low-fat natural yogurt
1 tbsp chopped fresh mint leaves

Takes 30 minutes • Serves 2

1 Trim the aubergine and cut lengthways into 6 thick slices. Season all over and brush with 2 tablespoons of the oil. Heat the remaining oil in a small pan and add the tomatoes, garlic and chilli flakes, along with a little salt. Cook gently for 3–4 minutes until the tomatoes are just softened. In a small bowl, mix the yogurt with the mint and some seasoning.
2 Cook the aubergine slices for 5–6 minutes on each side on a barbecue, in a griddle pan or under the grill on a medium–high heat, until nicely browned and softened. Serve three slices per person with the minty yogurt and tomato sauces.

• Per serving 230 kcalories, protein 6g, carbohydrate 11g, fat 18g, saturated fat 3g, fibre 5g, sugar 10g, salt 0.16g

Polenta is ground corn and an ideal carbohydrate for anyone on a wheat- or gluten-free diet.

Polenta bruschetta with tapenade

700ml/1¼ pint vegetable stock
140g/5oz instant polenta
2 tbsp chopped fresh basil
olive oil, for greasing and brushing
9 tsp (about ½ 190g jar)
olive tapenade
9 SunBlush or sun-dried tomatoes,
halved
100g/4oz mixed salad leaves,
to serve

Takes 40 minutes, plus 1 hour setting
Serves 6

1 Bring the stock to the boil in a pan, then reduce to a simmer. Stirring continuously, pour in the polenta in a steady stream and cook for 5 minutes until thickened. Stir in the basil and season. Spread over an oiled shallow baking tin measuring 24cm x 18cm. Leave to set for 1 hour.

2 Cut the polenta into nine rectangles, each 8cm x 6cm, then cut in half diagonally to make triangle shapes. Heat a griddle or barbecue until hot, brush each triangle with oil and cook for 4–5 minutes each side, until crisp and golden.

3 Top each triangle with ½ teaspoon of the tapenade and ½ a tomato. Serve warm on a bed of salad leaves.

• Per serving 198 kcalories, protein 4g, carbohydrate 20g, fat 12g, saturated fat 2g, fibre 1g, added sugar none, salt 0.97g

These tortillas can also be fried in a large pan, or cooked under a hot grill. Vary the fillings to suit your tastes.

Cheesey tortilla wrap

4 tortillas
85g/3oz cheddar, grated
4 sun-dried or SunBlush tomatoes
from a jar, roughly chopped
1 tbsp jalapeños chillies from a jar,
drained and chopped
a handful of fresh coriander leaves
salsa and avocado salad, to serve

Takes 10 minutes • Serves 2–4

1 Lay 2 tortillas side by side on a hot barbecue. Scatter over all of the ingredients, evenly, then top with remaining 2 tortillas. Cook for 3 minutes until slightly crisp and golden. Then, carefully, using a flat baking sheet, turn over the two-tortilla stacks. Cook on the other side for 3 minutes until the cheese has melted.
2 Slide off the barbecue using the baking sheet and cut into wedges. Great served with salsa, for dipping, and an avocado salad.

• Per serving (4) 248 kcalories, protein 10g, carbohydrate 34g, fat 9g, saturated fat 5g, fibre 2g, sugar 1g, salt 1.03g

This is a great vegetarian main course served with hot tortillas, which are easy to assemble into juicy, warm sandwiches.

BBQ vegetables with goat's cheese

4 aubergines, cut lengthways into
1cm slices
8 plum tomatoes, each cut into
3 thick slices
2 bunches of spring onions, trimmed
150ml/¼ pint extra virgin olive oil,
plus extra for drizzling
2 tbsp white wine vinegar
3 plump garlic cloves, crushed
2 x 100g packs firm goat's cheese
8 flour tortillas
a large handful of fresh basil leaves,
to serve

Takes 35–40 minutes • Serves 8

1 Put the sliced aubergines, tomatoes and whole spring onions into a large shallow dish. Whisk together the olive oil, white wine vinegar and garlic with plenty of seasoning, pour over the vegetables and toss well.
2 Remove the aubergine slices from the marinade and barbecue or grill over a medium–high heat for 4–5 minutes each side, until tender and marked. Remove and put into a large shallow bowl. Barbecue the tomatoes and spring onions for 3–4 minutes, turning once. Add to the aubergines. Crumble the goat's cheese over the hot vegetables, drizzle with extra virgin olive oil and toss.
3 Warm the tortillas on the barbecue for 1–2 minutes, turning (or according to the packet instructions) then serve with the warm vegetables, scattered with basil.

• Per serving 415 kcalories, protein 10g, carbohydrate 36g, fat 26g, saturated fat 3g, fibre 5g, added sugar 1g, salt 1.89g

Lightly toasting the cut sides of burger buns gives just a little crunch and stops them going soggy.

Garlic and mushroom burgers

4 portobello or field mushrooms, stalks trimmed
1 tsp sunflower oil
50g/2oz vegetarian gruyere, grated
1 garlic clove, crushed
1 tbsp butter, softened
4 ciabatta or burger buns, split and toasted
lettuce, tomatoes and sliced red onion, to serve

Takes 20 minutes • Serves 4

1 Heat a barbecue or grill to a medium–high heat. Rub the mushrooms with the oil then barbecue or grill for 3 minutes on each side until cooked but still firm.
2 Mix the cheese, garlic, butter and some seasoning in a bowl, then spoon into the mushrooms. Cook for another few minutes until the cheese begins to melt and then stuff into the toasted ciabatta or buns along with the salad.

• Per serving 228 kcalories, protein 11g, carbohydrate 23g, fat 11g, saturated fat 5g, fibre 3g, sugar 1g, salt 1.05g

Rather cook indoors? Just griddle for 3–4 minutes until charred.

Lemon and rosemary halloumi skewers

2 tbsp olive oil
1 fresh rosemary sprig, leaves chopped
1 large lemon, halved lengthways
250g pack halloumi cheese, cut into large chunks
1 small red onion, cut into 8 wedges
1 courgette, cut into 8 chunks
houmous and couscous, to serve

Takes 20 minutes, plus 15 minutes marinating • Serves 4

1 Mix the olive oil and rosemary in a non-metallic bowl. Grate the zest and squeeze the juice from ½ the lemon, then add to the mixture. Season to taste. Stir in the halloumi chunks to coat in the marinade. Cover, then leave to marinate for 15 minutes.
2 Cut the other half of the lemon into four wedges, then cut each wedge in half. Remove the halloumi from the marinade and thread onto 4 metal skewers with the red onion, lemon wedges and courgette. Barbecue for 5–10 minutes, turning occasionally and brushing on any leftover marinade. Serve with houmous and couscous.

• Per skewer 237 kcalories, protein 12g, carbohydrate 3g, fat 20g, saturated fat 9g, fibre 1g, sugar 2g, salt 2.06g

Roasting aubergines in the oven or on the barbecue lets them keep their shape for stuffing.

Stuffed aubergines with coriander yogurt dressing

1 medium aubergine
2 tsp olive oil
juice of 1 lemon, zest of ½
100g/4oz couscous
300ml/½ pint boiling vegetable stock
85g/3oz ready-to-eat dried apricots, roughly chopped
4 sun-dried tomatoes in oil, drained and chopped
3 spring onions, finely sliced
25g/1oz pine nuts, toasted
a pinch of ground cinnamon
leafy salad, to serve

FOR THE DRESSING
4 heaped tbsp Greek-style natural yogurt
2 tsp fresh lemon juice
1 fat garlic clove, crushed
a small knob of fresh root ginger, finely chopped
a small handful of fresh coriander, roughly chopped

Takes 45 minutes • Serves 2

1 Halve the aubergine lengthways and score the flesh deeply with a sharp knife in a criss-cross pattern. Mix the olive oil, lemon juice and some seasoning, and brush over the scored surface. Barbecue cut-side down, covered by an upturned roasting tin or with the barbecue lid down, for 15–20 minutes until tender.
2 Meanwhile, put the couscous and boiling stock in a large bowl and soak for 10 minutes until all stock is absorbed. Then stir in the apricots, tomatoes, spring onions, pine nuts and cinnamon.
3 Scoop out the aubergine flesh, keeping skins intact. Chop the flesh and add to the couscous with some seasoning. Pile a generous amount of the couscous in each skin, and any left over into a serving bowl. Whisk the dressing ingredients, and serve drizzled over each stuffed aubergine with a leafy salad on the side.

• Per serving 398 kcalories, protein 12g, carbohydrate 49g, fat 19g, saturated fat 4g, fibre 7g, added sugar none, salt 1.05g

Mix and match this salad with other canned beans, such as butter or flageolet. It also works well as an accompaniment to most barbecued or grilled meats and fish.

Warm chickpea salad

1 red onion, cut into wedges
2 courgettes, thickly sliced
1 red pepper, seeded and cut into large chunks
375g/13oz ripe tomatoes
5 tbsp olive oil
juice of ½ lemon
3 tbsp chopped/snipped fresh mixed herbs (such as chives, parsley and mint) or 3 tbsp fresh parsley
2 × 400g cans chickpeas, drained and rinsed
100g/4oz feta, cut into cubes

Takes 45 minutes • Serves 4

1 Thread the vegetables onto a few skewers, drizzle with a little of the olive oil and barbecue or grill on a medium–high heat, turning until the vegetables are softened and slightly charred – the tomatoes won't take long.
2 Meanwhile, mix the lemon juice and remaining olive oil to make a dressing. Season and stir in the herbs.
3 When the vegetables are cooked, cool for a few minutes, then pull the vegetables from the skewers, halving the tomatoes. Put into a bowl with the chickpeas, feta and dressing. Toss lightly before serving.

• Per serving 371 kcalories, protein 15g, carbohydrate 28g, fat 23g, saturated fat 5g, fibre 7g, added sugar none, salt 1.62g

To make life easier, you can prepare batches of these burgers and freeze them, uncooked, in stacks with a square of greaseproof paper between each one to stop them sticking together.

Cheesey veg burgers

2 tbsp olive oil
2 leeks, sliced
200g/8oz mushrooms, sliced
2 carrots, peeled and coarsely grated
1 tsp each cumin and mild chilli powder
1 tbsp soy sauce
300g can pinto or kidney beans, drained and rinsed
100g/4oz cheddar, grated
200g/8oz granary bread, torn into pieces
toasted burger buns, lettuce, tomato and favourites sauces, to serve

Takes 30 minutes • Serves 4

1 Heat half the oil in a pan then add the vegetables, spices and soy sauce, and cook, stirring occasionally, for 10 minutes until soft. Tip into a food processor with the beans, cheese and bread, season, then pulse to a thick paste.

2 With wet hands, mould the paste into 8 burgers. To cook, brush with a little of the remaining oil and barbecue or fry for 2–3 minutes on each side until crispy. Serve with the toasted buns and salad, as well as any favourites such as ketchup and mayo, on the side.

• Per serving 177 kcalories, protein 8g, carbohydrate 21g, fat 7g, saturated fat 3g, fibre 4g, added sugar 5g, salt 2.13g

Bulghar wheat has a lovely nutty flavour and texture – try swapping it for couscous in salads for a change.

Feta tabbouleh with aubergines

140g/5oz bulghar wheat
2 garlic cloves, crushed
4 tbsp olive oil
2 aubergines, thinly sliced lengthways
400g can chickpeas, drained
140g/5oz cherry tomatoes, halved
1 red onion, chopped
100g/4oz feta, crumbled
1 large bunch of fresh mint, leaves chopped
juice of 1½ lemons

Takes 30 minutes • Serves 4

1 Cook the bulghar wheat according to the packet instructions, then drain well. In a small bowl, mix together the garlic and olive oil, then use half to brush over both sides of the aubergine strips with some seasoning. Sear the strips on a hot barbecue, or frying pan for 3 minutes each side until charred and softened.

2 Tip the bulghar wheat into a large bowl with the chickpeas, tomatoes, onion, feta and mint, then pour over the remaining garlicky oil and the lemon juice. Mix and season well, then pile onto plates with the charred aubergines.

• Per serving 395 kcalories, protein 14g, carbohydrate 44g, fat 19g, saturated fat 5g, fibre 6g, sugar 7g, salt 1.29g

These little wedges are perfect as a starter while waiting for the rest of the barbecue fare. Try a mix of plain and flavoured pittas.

Crisp feta nibbles

6 pitta breads
200g pack feta
20g pack flat-leaf parsley or mint,
leaves roughly chopped
freshly ground black pepper, to taste
vegetable crudités, plus houmous,
tzatziki or your favourite dips,
to serve

Takes 15 minutes • Serves 6
(easily doubled)

1 Toast the pittas in a toaster until they're just under-done – puffed up but not yet crisp – then leave to cool for a few minutes. Meanwhile, using a fork, mash the feta in a large bowl. Stir in the herbs and lots of black pepper.
2 Cut a small slit along one edge of each pitta, then spoon in the feta. Spread it out over the inside of the bread with the back of the spoon or a cutlery knife.
3 To serve, re-toast the pittas, cut-side up (don't get cheese in the toaster!) or on the barbecue until the bread is just crisp, then leave to cool for 2 minutes before cutting into wedges. Best eaten within 30 minutes of toasting. Serve with a selection of dips.

• Per serving 277 kcalories, protein 12g, carbohydrate 42g, fat 8g, saturated fat 4g, fibre 2g, sugar 3g, salt 2.06g

This fresh-tasting salsa is an ideal match for barbecued meats and fish. Seasoning just before serving stops the salsa from becoming watery.

Tomato, cucumber and coriander salsa

6 vine-ripened tomatoes
1 small cucumber, seeded and finely diced
1 red onion, finely chopped
small bunch of fresh coriander, leaves chopped

Takes 15 minutes • Serves 6

1 Halve the tomatoes, scrape out the seeds and discard, and then finely chop the flesh. Mix the chopped tomatoes with the diced cucumber, onion and coriander, and chill until ready to serve. (You can chill for up to one day before seasoning and serving.)
2 Just before eating, add some seasoning. Give everything a final mix together and serve with burgers, barbecued chicken or fish.

• Per serving 34 kcalories, protein 2g, carbohydrate 6g, fat none, saturated fat none, fibre 2g, sugar 6g, salt 0.03g

You can happily make this dish the day before, chill it, then bring the salad back to room temperature and give it a good stir before serving.

Butter bean and tomato salad

420g can butter beans, drained
and rinsed
500g/1lb 2oz cherry tomatoes,
quartered
2 small green or yellow courgettes,
finely diced
1 small red onion, chopped
small bunch or fresh coriander,
chopped
2 tbsp fresh lemon juice
3 tbsp olive oil
1 tsp ground cumin

Takes 15–20 minutes • Serves 6–8

1 Tip all the ingredients into a bowl with some salt and pepper, and mix well. Cover and leave at room temperature until ready to serve.

• Per serving (6) 109 kcalories, protein 4g, carbohydrate 9g, fat 6g, saturated fat 1g, fibre 3g, added sugar none, salt 0.41g

All the flavours of an Italian spring are here, with a couple of British stalwarts – perfect for early English summer barbecues.

Spring salad with watercress dressing

550g/1lb 4oz new potatoes, scrubbed
200g/8oz shelled broad beans
200g/8oz fresh young asparagus
100g/4oz fresh peas
90g pack prosciutto, sliced into ribbons
125g bag mixed salad leaves
100g/4oz pecorino cheese, shaved

FOR THE DRESSING
50g/2oz fresh watercress, roughly chopped
6 tbsp extra virgin olive oil
2 tbsp cider vinegar
a pinch of sugar

Takes 30–35 minutes • Serves 4

1 Cook the potatoes in boiling salted water for 10–15 minutes until tender. Drain and halve when cool enough to handle. Blanch the beans and asparagus in boiling salted water for 2–3 minutes, adding the peas for the last minute. Drain in a sieve and cool under running cold water. Toss together the asparagus, beans, peas, potatoes and prosciutto.
2 For the dressing, put all the ingredients in a blender or food processor and blitz until really smooth and bright green, season.
3 To serve, toss the salad leaves with a spoonful or two of dressing and arrange on plates. Pile the vegetable mixture on top, season, then drizzle over the remaining dressing and scatter with the pecorino.

• Per serving 493 kcalories, protein 25g, carbohydrate 31g, fat 31g, saturated fat 9g, fibre 7g, added sugar 0.5g, salt 1.57g

An updated version of garlic bread, made wonderfully gooey with jarlsberg – a perennially popular accompaniment to summer salads or barbecues.

Cheesey garlic bread wedges

85g/3oz butter, at room temperature
2 garlic cloves, finely chopped
175g/6oz jarlsberg, coarsely grated
2 tbsp chopped parsley
¼ tsp crushed dried chillies
1 round French country loaf

Takes 35–45 minutes • Cuts into 12 wedges

1 Preheat the oven to 190°C/fan 170°C/Gas 5. Beat the butter and garlic, then mix in the cheese, parsley and chillies. Cut the bread in half crossways through the centre.
2 Spread the cheese mixture on the cut side of both bread halves. Wrap each half loosely in foil and put on a baking sheet. Bake for 20 minutes, then unwrap the foil and bake for a further 10–15 minutes, until pale golden. Cut into wedges and serve.

• Per wedge 152 kcals, protein 5g, carbohydate 10g, fat 10g, saturated fat 6g, fibre 1g, added sugar none, salt 0.92g

This yummy salad is an equally delicious barbecue accompaniment, served warm or cold.

Roast tomatoes with asparagus and black olives

750g/1lb 10oz cherry tomatoes
5 tbsp olive oil
6 garlic cloves, peeled and halved
24 asparagus spears
a handful of good black olives, stoned and chopped

Ready in 35–45 minutes • Serves 8

1 Preheat the oven to 200°C/fan 180°C/ Gas 6. Spread the tomatoes out on a large baking sheet and prick each with a fork. Sprinkle with 2 tablespoons of the olive oil, salt and pepper to taste, and scatter with the garlic. Roast in the oven for 15 minutes. Then remove and pour off the excess juice.
2 Meanwhile, lay the asparagus flat in a large frying pan over a medium heat. Splash with the remaining 3 tablespoons of olive oil and some seasoning, then just roll the spears until they're hot and evenly coated with oil. Push the tomatoes to one side of the baking sheet and tip in the asparagus next to them. Return to the oven and roast for 15 minutes. Sprinkle with the olives and serve.

• Per serving 102 kcalories, protein 3g, carbohydrate 5g, fat 8g, saturated fat 1g, fibre 2g, added sugar none, salt 0.18g

As there are no salad leaves to go droopy, this is a great idea for a bring-a-dish barbecue party.

Stir-fry noodle salad

250g or 4 blocks egg noodles
4 tbsp sesame oil
2 red peppers, seeded and finely sliced
2 carrots, sliced into batons
a large knob of fresh root ginger, finely chopped
2 garlic cloves, finely chopped
4 kaffir lime leaves, shredded
1 bunch spring onions, finely sliced
6 tbsp soy sauce
2 large handfuls of beansprouts
250g of tofu, cut into cubes
1 large bunch of fresh coriander, stalks finely chopped, leaves roughly chopped

FOR THE DRESSING
4 kaffir lime leaves
150ml/¼ pint rice wine vinegar
2 lemongrass stalks
1 small piece fresh red chilli (about ⅓)
2 tbsp golden caster sugar

Takes 25 minutes • Serves 6

1 To make the dressing, tip all the ingredients into a small pan and bring to a simmer. Boil for 1 minute, then remove from the heat to infuse.
2 Cook the noodles according to the packet instructions, then drain and toss with 3 tablespoons of the sesame oil. Leave to cool, tossing occasionally so they don't stick.
3 Heat the rest of the sesame oil in a wok and stir fry the peppers, carrots, ginger and garlic for 1 minute. To serve, tip the noodles into a bowl, with the lime leaves and remaining ingredients – reserving a handful of coriander. Drain over the dressing and toss together. Pile into a bowl and scatter with the remaining coriander.

• Per serving 301 kcalories, protein 10g, carbohydrate 44g, fat 11g, saturated fat 1g, fibre 3g, sugar 14g, salt 3.35g

Serve this simple salad as soon as you've poured over the dressing – wonderful with sizzling barbecued chicken or lamb kebabs or burgers.

Courgette salad

2 large courgettes
3 tbsp olive oil
1 tbsp fresh lemon or lime juice
1 tbsp clear honey
2 tsp poppy seeds
1 garlic clove, crushed

Takes 10 minutes • Serves 4

1 Coarsely grate the courgettes and tip into a serving bowl. Whisk together the remaining ingredients with some seasoning in a small jug to make the dressing.
2 To serve, stir the dressing into the courgettes.

• Per serving 117 kcalories, protein 2.5g, carbohydrate 5.5g, fat 9.6g, saturated fat 1.4g, fibre 1.1g, sugar 4.9g, salt 0.01g

You can prepare these potato parcels the day before, then simply barbecue before serving or bake in a hot oven.

Hot and spicy sweet potatoes

2 large sweet potatoes, peeled
4 tbsp olive oil
2 tbsp fresh thyme leaves, plus 2 fresh thyme sprigs
1 red chilli, seeded and finely chopped

Takes 1 hour • Serves 6

1 Cut the sweet potatoes crossways into slices 2.5cm thick. Lay each potato on a large sheet of foil, keeping the slices together. Drizzle with the olive oil, sprinkle with the thyme leaves, and about half of the chopped chilli, and season with plenty of salt and pepper. With your hands, massage the flavourings into each slice. Replace the slices on the foil as before. Lay a thyme sprig across the top of each potato and sprinkle with the remaining chilli. Wrap the foil securely around the potatoes to make two parcels.
2 Put the foil parcels on the rack over the hottest part of the barbecue or in an oven preheated to 220°C/fan 200°C/ Gas 7, and cook for 45 minutes until the potatoes are buttery and soft – unwrap and test with the point of a knife to check if they're ready.

• Per serving 132 kcalories, protein 1g, carbohydrate 16g, fat 8g, saturated fat 1g, fibre 2g, added sugar none, salt 0.08g

Vary this protein-packed salad each time you make it by using different coloured lentils or a mixture them.

Lentil and red pepper salad

400g can lentils, rinsed and drained
5 roasted red peppers from a jar, chopped
a handful of radishes, sliced
a handful of pitted olives
2 tbsp balsamic vinegar
4 tbsp olive oil
2 Little Gem lettuces
150–200g/6–8oz feta, crumbled

Takes 15 minutes • Serves 4

1 Tip the lentils and peppers into a bowl with the radishes, olives, vinegar and oil, and mix well. Season to taste. The lentil mixture can be chilled for up to a day before assembling with the rest of the ingredients to serve.
2 Separate the lettuce leaves and arrange over a large plate. Spoon over the lentil salad and scatter with the feta.

• Per serving 634 kcalories, protein 22g, carbohydrate 29g, fat 49g, saturated fat 14g, fibre 9g, sugar 12g, salt 6.81g

This refreshing salad goes perfectly with fish or chicken, marinated in aromatic Asian flavours.

Thai cucumber salad with sour chilli dressing

1 cucumber
1 Little Gem lettuce, shredded
140g/5oz beansprouts
bunch of fresh coriander, leaves roughly chopped
bunch of fresh mint, leaves roughly chopped

FOR THE DRESSING
1 tsp rice wine vinegar
1 tbsp fish sauce
½ tsp light muscovado sugar
2 red chillies, seeded and finely chopped

Takes 10 minutes • Serves 4

1 Mix the dressing ingredients together, stirring until the sugar dissolves.
2 Using a vegetable peeler, 'peel' strips from the cucumber, dropping into a large serving bowl.
3 Add the rest of the salad ingredients into the bowl, then pour over the dressing, mixing well to combine. Serve immediately.

• Per serving 27 kcalories, protein 2g, carbohydrate 4g, fat 1g, saturated fat none, fibre 1g, sugar 3g, salt 0.75g

Once you've tossed the potatoes in the dressing, cover the bowl and the potatoes should keep warm for up to an hour while waiting for the rest of the food to catch up.

Herbed potato salad

800g/1lb 12oz waxy new potatoes, such as Charlotte or Anya
4 tsp Dijon mustard
4 tsp white wine vinegar
4 tbsp olive oil
2 tbsp each snipped/chopped fresh chives, parsley and tarragon
a bed of green salad leaves, to serve

Takes 30–35 minutes • Serves 4

1 Steam or boil the whole potatoes for about 10–15 minutes or until tender when pierced. Remove and set aside to cool a little.
2 Mix the mustard and vinegar in a big serving bowl until smooth, add the oil and season to taste, if you want, then mix again until blended.
3 Halve or slice the potatoes and toss together with the herbs in the bowl of dressing. Serve on a bed of salad leaves.

• Per serving 252 kcalories, protein 4g, carbohydrate 33g, fat 12g, saturated fat 2g, fibre 2g, added sugar none, salt 0.44g

Wild rice has a slightly firmer texture than other varieties and looks pretty mixed with them, adding colour to your al fresco feast.

Wild rice and feta salad

250g/9oz mixed basmati and wild rice
400g can chickpeas, drained
100g pack dried cranberries
1 red onion, sliced
1 garlic clove, crushed
3 tbsp olive oil
2 tbsp fresh lemon juice
200g pack reduced-fat feta
a handful of flat-leaf parsley leaves, roughly chopped

Takes 30 minutes • Serves 4

1 Rinse the rice and then boil it according to the packet instructions, adding the chickpeas for the final 4 minutes. Drain and allow to cool a little, then mix through the cranberries and onion.
2 Whisk together the garlic, olive oil, lemon juice and seasoning to make a dressing. Toss with the rice mixture and pile onto a large serving plate. Crumble over the feta, then scatter with the chopped parsley. Serve warm or cold.

• Per serving 519 kcalories, protein 20g, carbohydrate 79g, fat 16g, saturated fat 5g, fibre 4g, sugar 19g, salt 1.82g

Roasting your own peppers is really easy and they can be healthier than shop-bought pre-roasted peppers, which are often stored in oil.

Grilled and marinated summer vegetables

4 red peppers
3 aubergines, cut into finger-thick rounds
3 courgettes, cut diagonally into finger-thick slices
4 red onions, cut into finger-thick slices
large bunch of flat-leaf parsley, chopped
2 garlic cloves, crushed

FOR THE DRESSING
5 tbsp sherry vinegar
100ml/3½fl oz olive oil

Takes 50 minutes • Serves 10

1 Whisk the dressing ingredients and some seasoning in a large bowl. Heat a griddle pan or frying pan over a high heat and blacken the peppers on all sides. Put in a bowl and cover with a plate until cool to touch.
2 Griddle the other vegetables, without oiling, until charred on all sides and softening. As they are done, toss them straight into the dressing, separating the onions into rings. Peel the peppers, reserving the juices in the bowl, seed and cut into strips. Toss in with the rest of the vegetables, then strain over the juices. Leave everything to cool, then season.
3 The salad can be kept in the fridge for 2 days, but remove a few hours before serving to bring it to room temperature. Stir through the parsley and garlic before serving.

• Per serving 138 kcalories, protein 3g, carbohydrate 10g, fat 10g, saturated fat 1g, fibre 4g, sugar 8g, salt 0.02g

It's worth using a really good-quality, fruity olive oil in this salad, as it really brings out the best of the tomatoes.

Tomato and mint salad

400g/14oz cherry tomatoes, halved
1 small red onion, finely chopped
a handful of fresh mint leaves
extra virgin olive oil, for drizzling
zest of 1 lemon

Takes 10 minutes • Serves 6

1 Arrange the halved tomatoes over a large plate or serving platter. Scatter over the onion, then tear over the mint leaves. This can be kept covered for 3–4 hours.
2 Just before serving, drizzle with some good extra virgin olive oil and season well. Finely scatter over the lemon zest and serve with other Italian-inspired barbecue fare.

• Per serving 62 kcalories, protein 1g, carbohydrate 3g, fat 5g, saturated fat 1g, fibre 1g, added sugar none, salt 0.02g

Corn on the cob is a classic but fiddly barbecue accompaniment – no messy cobs here, though, instead a Mexican-inspired salad that's ideal with spicy chicken or ribs.

Tortilla and bean salad

1 tbsp vegetable oil
180g can sweetcorn, drained
180g can kidney beans, drained and rinsed
225g bag mixed green salad leaves
a handful of plain tortilla chips
50ml/2oz soured cream
a pinch of sugar
zest and juice of 1 lime

Takes 15 minutes • Serves 6

1 Heat the oil in a frying pan and, when hot, stir in the sweetcorn. Cook for 3 minutes, stirring often until the corn is browned, then remove and leave to cool.
2 In a large serving bowl, toss together the sweetcorn, kidney beans, salad leaves and tortilla chips.
3 Mix together the soured cream, sugar and lime zest and juice in a small bowl to make a dressing. Drizzle the dressing over the salad and serve.

• Per serving 109 kcalories, protein 3g, carbohydrate 14g, fat 5g, saturated fat 1g, fibre 2g, added sugar 2g, salt 0.46g

Push the couscous to the side of the bowl once you've added the water – it should stop the grains at the bottom becoming soggy.

Tricolore couscous salad

200g/8oz couscous
2 tsp vegetable stock powder (or use a crumbled cube)
250g pack cherry tomatoes, halved
2 avocados, peeled, stoned and chopped
150g pack mozzarella, drained and chopped
a handful of rocket or young spinach leaves

FOR THE DRESSING
1 rounded tbsp pesto
1 tbsp fresh lemon juice
3 tbsp olive oil

Takes 15 minutes • Serves 4

1 Mix the couscous and stock in a bowl, pour over 300ml of boiling water, then cover with a plate and leave for 5 minutes.
2 For the dressing, mix the pesto with the lemon juice and some seasoning, then gradually mix in the oil. Pour over the couscous and mix with a fork.
3 Stir the tomatoes, avocados and mozzarella into the couscous, then lightly stir in the rocket or spinach to serve.

• Per serving 456 kcalories, protein 13g, carbohydrate 30g, fat 32g, saturated fat 8g, fibre 3g, sugar 3g, salt 0.60g

The perfect drink for a hot summer's day.

Really easy lemonade

3 lemons, roughly chopped
140g/5oz caster sugar
1 litre/1¾ pints cold water
plain or fruity-slice ice cubes,
to serve

Takes 10 minutes • Serves 4

1 Tip the lemons, sugar and half the water into a food processor and blend until the lemon is finely chopped.
2 Pour the mixture into a sieve over a bowl, then press through as much juice as you can. Top up with the remaining water and serve with plain ice cubes or water frozen with slices of lemon and lime.

• Per serving 140 kcalories, protein none, carbohydrate 37g, fat none, saturated fat none, fibre none, sugar 37g, salt 0.1g

You don't need an ice-cream machine to get that gorgeous velvety texture with this recipe – though if you have one, do use it.

Blueberry, coconut and lime ice cream

2 limes
140g/5oz golden caster sugar
125g punnet blueberries, plus extra to serve
200ml carton coconut cream
284ml pot double cream

Takes 20–25 minutes, plus a few hours freezing • Serves 4–6

1 Finely grate the zest from one of the limes and squeeze the juice from both. Put in a small pan with the sugar and heat gently, stirring to dissolve. Add the blueberries and simmer for 2 minutes, just until the skins split. Pour into a bowl and stir in the coconut cream. Cool.
2 Whip the cream until it just holds its shape, then gradually stir in the blueberry mixture. Put the ice-cream mixture in the freezer for about 1 hour, until it is set about 3cm in from the edge.
3 Remove and mix it all together using a whisk. When it's fairly smooth, return to the freezer for a further hour, then repeat the whisking one more time. Transfer the ice cream to a rigid container, cover and freeze until firm, or for up to a month. Before serving, move the ice cream to the fridge for 30 minutes to soften it. Serve with extra blueberries scattered over.

• Per serving (6) 429 kcalories, protein 3g, carbohydrate 29g, fat 35g, saturated fat 24g, fibre 1g, added sugar 25g, salt 0.05g

You'll find vin santo, a dessert wine from Tuscany, in Italian delis. Or use another sweet dessert wine.

Strawberry parfait with vin santo, mascarpone and biscotti

250g box biscotti biscuits
100ml/3½fl oz vin santo or other sweet dessert wine
400g punnet strawberries, hulled and halved
50g/2oz golden caster sugar
250g tub mascarpone
284ml pot double cream

Takes 25–30 minutes • Serves 6

1 Place the biscotti biscuits in a plastic bag and crush lightly with the end of a rolling pin, leaving them slightly chunky. Tip them into a bowl, drizzle over the vin santo and give a stir. In a small bowl, use a fork to slightly mash half of the strawberries with the sugar.
2 Whip the mascarpone with the double cream in a medium bowl, until it just holds its shape. In a 1-litre glass bowl, spread half of the soaked biscotti. Top with half of the mashed strawberries and then half of the mascarpone mixture. Repeat until you have used up everything, finishing with a layer of the mascarpone mixture. Slice the remaining strawberries and scatter over the top. Chill before serving.

• Per serving 660 kcalories, protein 5g, carbohydrate 52g, fat 48g, saturated fat 28g, fibre 1g, added sugar 18g, salt 0.58g

A super-speedy way to jazz up shop-bought ice cream for a sweet end to an impromptu summer barbecue.

Banana sundaes with fudge sauce

500ml tub banana ice cream
2 ripe bananas, sliced
a small handful of pecan nuts,
toasted and roughly chopped

FOR THE FUDGE SAUCE
50g/2oz butter
5 tbsp soft brown sugar
142ml pot double cream

Takes 5 minutes • Serves 4

1 To make the sauce, melt together the butter, sugar and cream in a small pan over a low heat. Increase the heat and bubble for a couple of minutes, stirring, until you have a smooth, shiny sauce. Transfer to a jug and allow to cool.
2 To serve, layer the banana ice cream in four glasses with the banana slices and some of the fudge sauce. Top with a final glug of sauce and scatter with a few pecans.

• Per serving 637 kcalories, protein 6g, carbohydrate 62.4g, fat 42.1g, saturated fat 24.1g, fibre 0.7g, sugar 59.9g, salt 0.42g

This is a lighter, sparkling alternative to red wine – just perfect for outdoor summer drinking.

Refreshing red wine cooler

750ml bottle fruity red wine (Rioja
is good)
600ml/1 pint lemonade
1 lemon
a few fresh mint sprigs

Takes 5 minutes • Serves 8

1 Chill the red wine and lemonade until you are about to use it. Thinly slice the lemon.
2 When you are ready to serve, simply stir together the wine and lemonade in a large jug. Pour into glasses garnishing with the slices of lemon and some mint leaves.

• Per serving 83 kcalories, protein 0.2g, carbohydrate 4.9g, fat none, saturated fat none, fibre none, sugar 4.9g, salt 0.03g

Dairy free, this ice gets its smooth texture from the addition of coconut cream.

Pineapple and coconut ice with poached pineapple

1 large and 1 medium golden
pineapple
juice of 3 limes
175g/6oz golden icing sugar, sifted
200ml carton coconut cream

FOR THE SYRUP
100g/4oz golden caster sugar
1 cinnamon stick
fresh mint leaves, to serve

Takes 50 minutes, plus freezing time
Serves 6

1 Peel the large pineapple, halve, then quarter lengthways. Cut out and discard the central woody core. Roughly chop the remaining flesh then whiz in a food processor to a rough purée. Stir in the lime juice, sugar and coconut cream. Freeze in a bowl for 2–3 hours until set about 3cm in from the edge, remove and whisk to break down the large ice crystals. Freeze for a further 1–2 hours until firm.

2 Peel the second pineapple and thinly slice. Gently heat the sugar, cinnamon and 2 tablespoons of water in a pan until the sugar dissolves, then boil to a light syrup. Add the pineapple and cook for 2–3 minutes, turning, until it intensifies in colour. Remove from the heat and cool.

3 Half an hour before serving, transfer the ice to the fridge. Serve with the sliced pineapple and scatter with mint leaves and pieces of cinnamon from the syrup.

• Per serving 397 kcalories, protein 2g, carbohydrate 75g, fat 12g, saturated fat 10g, fibre 3g, added sugar 48g, salt trace

Making your own jelly using a good-quality smoothie means a lot more flavour and a lot less sugar.

Smoothie jellies with ice cream

6 gelatine leaves
1-litre bottle orange, mango and passion fruit smoothie

TO SERVE
500ml tub good-quality vanilla ice cream

Takes 1 hour 5 minutes • Makes 12 mini or 6 large pots

1 Put the leaf gelatine in a bowl and cover with cold water. Leave for a few minutes until soft and floppy. Meanwhile, gently heat the smoothie in a pan without boiling. Take off the heat. Lift the gelatine out the water, squeeze out the excess water, then add to the smoothie pan. Stir well until melted, then pour into 6 or 12 moulds, pots or glasses and chill for at least 1 hour to set.

2 Serve each smoothie jelly topped with ice cream. For perfect mini scoops of ice cream, dip a tablespoon into a cup of hot water, then shake off the excess water. Scoop the ice cream, dipping the spoon in the hot water each time.

• Per serving (12) 92 kcalories, protein 4g, carbohydrate 15g, fat 2g, saturated fat 1g, fibre 2g, sugar 13g, salt 0.05g

Once made, this is a great stand-by that can be pulled out at a moment's notice.

Frozen banana and peanut butter cheesecake

3 small bananas
50g/2oz butter, melted
10 digestive biscuits, crushed to crumbs
142ml pot double cream
140g/5oz icing sugar
400g tub soft cheese
½ tsp vanilla extract
237g jar crunchy peanut butter

Takes 30 minutes, plus freezing
Serves 8–10

1 Freeze two bananas until the skins go black, then remove the skins and defrost the flesh so you are left with really soft bananas. Mash and set aside.

2 Mix the butter and biscuits together and press into a 22cm springform cake tin. Whip the cream until it just holds its shape. In another bowl, beat together the sugar, soft cheese and vanilla until smooth. Finally, beat the peanut butter to loosen it.

3 Fold the cream-cheese mix into the peanut butter with the mashed banana, then gently fold in the cream. Spread over the biscuit base, smoothing the surface. Freeze for a few hours or preferably overnight. To serve, move to the fridge for 20 minutes, then run a knife around the side and remove the tin. Slice the remaining banana to decorate.

• Per serving (8) 624 kcalories, protein 12g, carbohydrate 43g, fat 46g, saturated fat 21g, fibre 3g, sugar 30g, salt 1.18g

This sparkling wine cocktail is a lovely way to begin an evening. Don't hesitate to double up on the quantities, as your guests are bound to want more than one glass.

Sparkling mint and lemon juleps

85g/3oz golden caster sugar
4 tbsp fresh lemon juice

TO SERVE
1 x 75cl bottle chilled sparkling wine,
cava is a good choice
20g pack fresh mint

Takes 15 minutes, plus cooling
Serves 6

1 Put the sugar and lemon juice in a small pan and heat gently to dissolve the sugar. Simmer for 2 minutes to make a syrup. Remove from the heat and leave to cool. This can be made in advance and kept in the fridge for up to a week.
2 Pour the lemon syrup into six champagne flutes or tall glasses, top up each glass with the chilled sparkling wine, then stir quickly to mix before serving with mint sprigs tucked into the top.

• Per serving 149 kcalories, protein 11g, carbohydrate 21.5g, fat none, saturated fat none, fibre none, sugar 21.4g, salt 0.02g

The dimpled apricots look charming left whole, but you can halve and stone them before poaching if you prefer.

Summery Provençal apricots

1 × 75cl bottle fruity rosé wine
175g/6oz golden caster sugar
1 vanilla pod, split open lengthways
with a sharp knife, then cut into 4
(keep the seeds inside)
700g/1lb 9oz ripe fresh apricots
vanilla ice cream, to serve

Takes 35–45 minutes • Serves 4

1 Pour the wine into a pan with the sugar and pieces of vanilla pod. Stir over a low heat until the sugar dissolves, then add the apricots. Cover and gently poach until just softened – about 15–20 minutes for whole fruit and 10–15 minutes for halves.
2 Lift out the apricots and put them in a bowl. Boil the liquid hard for 8–10 minutes to make a thin syrup. Pour over the apricots and leave to cool. Serve warm or cold with a good vanilla ice cream and a piece of vanilla pod to decorate.

• Per serving 356 kcalories, protein 2g, carbohydrate 62g, fat none, saturated fat 3g, fibre 3g, added sugar 46g, salt 0.03g

The perfect pud for a get-together – simply melt, mix, and stick it in the fridge.

Quick chocolate and nut cake

100g/4oz butter
400g/14oz plain chocolate
50g/2oz sugar
½ tsp ground cinnamon
200g/8oz macaroons or coconut biscuits, broken into pieces
100g/4oz Brazil nuts, roughly chopped
desiccated coconut, to decorate

Takes 20 minutes, plus chilling
Serves 6

1 Line a 900g loaf tin with a double layer of cling film. Melt the butter, chocolate and sugar in a bowl set over a pan of simmering water over a low heat. Stir in the cinnamon, macaroons or coconut biscuits and nuts.
2 Pour the mixture into the prepared tin, smooth over the surface with a knife and cover completely with cling film. Leave in the fridge to set for at least two hours.
3 To serve, set on a plate, remove the cling film and sprinkle with the desiccated coconut. The cake is fairly rich, so slice it into thin pieces and serve with fresh fruit or ice cream, if you like.

• Per serving 759 kcalories, protein 9g, carbohydrate 73g, fat 50g, saturated fat 22g, fibre 3g, added sugar 70g, salt 0.32g

Instead of blueberries, try raspberries and redcurrants, or chopped strawberries – most summer berries will do.

Blueberry and lime cheesecake

300g/10oz sweet oaty biscuits, crumbed
100g/4oz butter, melted
500g/1lb 2oz blueberries
225g/8½oz golden caster sugar
grated zest and juice of 2 limes
2 × 250g tubs Quark
284ml pot double cream
284ml pot soured cream
4 tsp powdered gelatine

Takes 1 hour, plus chilling • Serves 8

1 Heat the oven to 180°C/fan 160°C/Gas 4 and line the base of a 23cm springform tin. Mix the biscuit crumbs and butter. Press evenly into the tin and bake for 10 minutes until crisp. Cool.

2 Cook a third of the blueberries, 175g of the sugar, the zest of 1 lime and 3 tablespoons of water in a pan for 2 minutes until the berries start to burst. Cool. Strain the juice into a pan, reserving the cooked berries.

3 Beat the Quark and creams with the remaining sugar, lime zest and juice until smooth. Sprinkle the gelatine over 3 tablespoons of water. Leave until spongy, then dissolve until clear over a pan of water on a low heat. Beat some cream mixture into the gelatine then stir back into the rest of the mixture. Lightly fold in the cooked berries. Spoon over the biscuit base. Chill for 4 hours or until set.

4 Meanwhile boil the reserved juice for 2 minutes until syrupy. Stir in the remaining berries and cool. When set, carefully remove the cake on to a plate and spoon over the syrupy berries.

• Per serving 689 kcalories, protein 16g, carbohydrate 63g, fat 44g, saturated fat 26g, fibre 1g, added sugar 37g, salt 0.75g

This fruity recipe is easy to make but looks special enough for entertaining.

Fruity shortcake swirl

4 tbsp lemon curd
200g pot Greek yogurt
250g pot virtually fat-free fromage frais
400g/14oz strawberries, hulled
8 shortbread rounds, roughly crumbled

Takes 15–20 minutes • Serves 4

1 Mix together the lemon curd, yogurt and fromage frais. Roughly mash the strawberries, then gently stir them through the lemon mixture.

2 Drop half the shortbread into four glasses and top with half the fruit yogurt. Sprinkle over the remaining shortbread and finish with the rest of the fruit yogurt.

• Per serving 283 kcalories, protein 10g, carbohydrate 36g, fat 12g, saturated fat 7g, fibre 2g, added sugar 9g, salt 0.33g

The perfect ending to a perfect summer barbecue.

Classic summer pudding

300g/10oz strawberries, hulled
and quartered
250g/9oz blackberries
100g/4oz each blackcurrants and
redcurrants
500g/1lb 2oz raspberries
175g/6oz golden caster sugar
7 slices square medium-cut white
sliced loaf (day-old is best),
crusts removed
extra berries and cream, to serve

Takes 30 minutes, plus chilling
Serves 8

1 Wash the fruit and gently dry on kitchen paper, keeping the strawberries separate. Gently heat the sugar and 3 tablespoons of water in a large pan until the sugar dissolves. Bring to the boil for 1 minute, then tip in all but the strawberries and cook for 3 minutes over a low heat. Sieve the fruit, reserving the juice.
2 Line a medium pudding basin with two sheets of overlapping cling film. Dip 1 slice of bread in the fruit juices and push into the bottom of the basin. Halve 4 slices of bread diagonally, dip, and press around the basin's sides so they fit together neatly. Now spoon in the fruit, adding the strawberries as you go. Dip the final bread and patch together to cover the surface. Wrap with cling film, top with a plate weighed down with some tins and chill for 6 hours or overnight.
3 Serve turned out on to a serving plate, dribbled with any leftover juice, extra berries and cream.

• Per serving 248 kcalories, protein 6g, carbohydrate 57g, fat 1g, saturated fat none, fibre 9g, added sugar 43g, salt 0.45g

Keep the kids happy with this colourful cooler.

Non-alcoholic tropical fizz

500ml/18fl oz apple juice
500ml/18fl oz tropical fruit juice
500ml/18fl oz soda water
a handful of strawberries, hulled
and halved
1 kiwi fruit, peeled and chopped
2 pineapple rings, chopped

Takes 10 minutes • Serves 8

1 Chill the juices and soda water. Mix together the fruit and divide among eight glasses, cover and chill.
2 To serve, stir together the juices and soda water in a large jug until well mixed. Pour over the chopped fruit and serve immediately.

• Per serving 62 kcalories, protein 0.6g, carbohydrate 15.6g, fat 0.1g, saturated fat none, fibre 0.5g, sugar 15.6g, salt 0.01g

The fragrance of the basil works really well with the scented peaches.
Serve warm from the pan with scoops of good vanilla ice cream.

Warm peaches with basil and honey

25g/1oz unsalted butter
2 ripe peaches or nectarines, stoned
and thickly sliced
2 tbsp clear honey
juice of 1 orange
8–10 fresh basil leaves, shredded
vanilla or white chocolate ice cream,
to serve

Takes 10 minutes • Serves 4

1 Melt the butter in a large frying pan and add the peaches or nectarines. Cook for a couple of minutes on both sides until slightly softened.
2 Add the honey and stir to make a sauce, then add the orange juice and allow to bubble briefly. Stir in the basil and serve warm with scoops of ice cream.

• Per serving (without ice cream) 101 kcalories, protein 1g, carbohydrate 13g, fat 5g, saturated fat 3g, fibre 1g, added sugar 6g, salt 0.01g

A stunning pudding that is great for entertaining as it can be made ahead – just remember to transfer it to the fridge before eating or it will be too icy to slice.

Mango, lime and blackberry bombe

2 × 200g punnets blackberries
250g/9oz icing sugar
2 × 425g cans mango in syrup, juice reserved
grated zest and juice of 4 limes
142ml pot and 285ml pot double cream
2 shop-bought brandy snaps, crushed to serve

Takes 30 minutes, plus freezing
Serves 10

1 Cook the berries, 4 tablespoons of the sugar and a splash of water in a pan until the berries soften. Push the fruit through a sieve, cool, then freeze until slushy, stirring every now and then.
2 Whiz the mango with 75ml of its syrup and a further 2 tablespoons of the sugar until smooth, then freeze until slushy, as above.
3 Stir the lime zest and juice into the remaining sugar. Beat both pots of cream with 3 tablespoons of the remaining mango syrup until soft peaks form, then beat in the lime sugar. Freeze until semi-frozen.
4 Line a medium basin with cling film then beat all three icy mixtures and spoon alternately into the bowl to make rippled layers. Freeze until solid.
5 To serve, tip out of the bowl on to a plate and remove the cling film. Scatter with the crushed biscuits and soften for 30 minutes in the fridge before eating.

• Per serving 400 kcalories, protein 1g, carbohydrate 48g, fat 23g, saturated fat 13g, fibre 2g, sugar 47g, salt 0.06g

Index

apricots, summery Provençal
196–7
asparagus and black olives, roast
tomatoes with 154–5
aubergines
feta tabbouleh with 142–3
smoky salad 66–7
stuffed 136–7
with yogurt and tomato
sauces 124–5
avocado salsa, chunky 112–13

bananas
and peanut butter
cheesecake, frozen 192–3
sundaes with fudge sauce
184–5
basil 108–9, 208–9
beans
butter, and tomato salad
148–9
and tortilla salad 174–5
beef
classic 48–9
herby, and couscous burgers
76–7
open burgers with beetroot
70–1
oriental skewers with
cucumber salad 54–5

see also steak
beetroot
open burgers with 70–1
warm salad 68–9
biscotti 182–3
blackberry, mango and lime
bombe 210–11
blueberry
coconut and lime ice cream
180–1
and lime cheesecake 200–1
burgers
cheesey veg 140–1
classic beef 48–9
falafel 6, 7, 118–19
garlic and mushroom 132–3
herby beef and couscous
76–7
open, with beetroot 70–1
sticky sausage with cheese
10–11
tangy tuna 106–7
Thai-spiced chicken 32–3

cake, quick chocolate and nut
198–9
cheese
blue, and hot steak wrap 52–3
garlic bread wedges 152–3
goat's, BBQ vegetables with

130–1
mozzarella and prosciutto
panini 26–7
sticky sausage burgers with
10–11
tortilla wraps 128–9
veg burgers 140–1
see also feta; halloumi
cheesecake
blueberry and lime 200–1
frozen banana and peanut
butter 192–3
chicken
Cajun 40–1
griddled mezze 16–17
herbed skewers 42–3
lime and pepper wraps 36–7
mango, rice and peas with
12–13
pan-roasted, with crisp
prosciutto and tomatoes
24–5
red curry kebabs 22–3
spatchcock barbecue 28–9
spicy yogurt 46–7
Thai-spiced burgers 32–3
zesty ginger 20–1
chickpeas 118–19
chorizo and squid salad 96–7
lemon and parsley, sardines

with 80–1
  warm salad 138–9
chilli 92–3, 94–5, 164–5
chocolate and nut cake 198–9
chorizo, squid, and chickpea
  salad 96–7
coconut
  lime and blueberry ice cream
    180–1
  and pineapple ice with
    poached pineapple 188–9
coriander 136–7, 146–7
  courgette salads 100–1,
    158–9
  couscous 76–7, 176–7
  cucumbers 146–7, 164–5
  curry, red, chicken kebabs
    22–3

dressings 170–1, 176–7
  coriander yogurt 136–7
  sour chilli 164–5
  sun-dried tomato 58–9
  watercress 150–1

falafel burgers 6, 7, 118–19
fennel salad, Sicilian 104–5
feta
  crisp nibbles 144–5
  peas and mint, charred lamb
    with 50–1
  tabbouleh with aubergines
    142–3
  toasty kebabs 120–1
  and wild rice salad 168–9
fish 88–9
  grilled, with chunky avocado

salsa 112–13
  lemony parcels 102–3
  tikka-style 86–7
  see also salmon; sardines; sea
    bass; tuna
fudge sauce 184–5

garlic 132–3, 152–3
ginger 20–1, 94–5, 110–11

haddock, lemony 102–3
halloumi
  lemon and rosemary skewers
    134–5
  and pepper, wraps 122–3
  watermelon and mint salad
    116–17
honey 208–9
hotdogs, Cumberland, with
    charred tomato salsa 44–5
houmous, BBQ lamb with 60–1

ice cream
  blueberry, coconut and lime
    180–1
  smoothie jellies with 190–1

juleps, sparkling mint and lemon
    194–5

kebabs
  pork, lemon and potato 30–1
  pork and peach 14–15
  red curry chicken 22–3
  Thai salmon 92–3
  toasty feta 120–1

lamb
  BBQ, with houmous 60–1
  charred, with peas, mint and
    feta 50–1
  chops, with smoky aubergine
    salad 66–7
  kofta pitta pockets 56–7
  minty kebabs 62–3
  sizzled steaks, with warm
    beetroot salad 68–9
  sizzling, with Mexican salsa
    74–5
  Turkish-style 78–9
lemon
  drinks with 194–5
  mains with 30–1, 38–9, 80–1,
    102–3, 134–5
lemonade, really easy 178–9
lemongrass 110–11
lentil and red pepper salad 162–3
lime
  desserts with 180–1, 200–1,
    210–11
  mains with 36–7, 92–3, 94–5

mackerel
  barbecued, with ginger, chilli
    and lime drizzle 94–5
  spiced toasts 82–3
mango
  chicken, rice and peas with
    12–13
  lime and blackberry bombe
    210–11
  salsa, seared swordfish with
    88–9
marinades 28–9, 30–1

mascarpone 182–3
mayonnaise, basil 108–9
mint
    drinks with 194–5
    mains with 50–1, 62–3,
        116–17, 172–3
mozzarella and prosciutto panini
    26–7
mushrooms
    and garlic burgers 132–3
    porcini-rubbed steak 72–3

noodle salad 18–19, 156–7
nut and chocolate cake 198–9

olives, black 154–5
onion, caramelised 64–5

panini, mozzarella and prosciutto
    26–7
parfait, strawberry 182–3
parsley 80–1
    salad 114–15
peaches
    and pork kebabs 14–15
    warm 208–9
peanut butter and banana
    cheesecake, frozen 192–3
peas 12–13, 50–1
peppers
    and halloumi, roasted, wraps
        122–3
    and lime chicken wraps 36–7
    red, and lentil salad 162–3
pineapple and coconut ice with
    poached pineapple 188–9
pittas

crisp feta nibbles 144–5
    kofta pockets 56–7
    Turkish-style lamb 78–9
polenta bruschetta with tapenade
    126–7
pork
    Asian, with rice noodle salad
        18–19
    lemon and potato kebabs
        30–1
    and peach kebabs with Little
        Gem salad 14–15
    with sage, lemon and
        prosciutto, barbecued 38–9
    sticky sausage burgers with
        cheese 10–11
potatoes
    herbed salad 166–7
    pork and lemon kebabs 30–1
    and tomatoes, peppery 84–5
prawns
    bay-scented, with basil
        mayonnaise 108–9
    piri-piri 90–1
prosciutto 24–5, 26–7, 38–9

rice
    and peas with mango chicken
        12–13
    red curry chicken kebabs
        22–3
    wild, and feta salad 168–9
rice noodle salad 18–19
rosemary 134–5

sage 38–9
salad

butter bean and tomato 148–9
chargrilled courgettes and
    salmon 100–1
courgette 158–9
cucumber 54–5
halloumi, watermelon and mint
    116–17
herbed potato 166–7
lentil and red pepper 162–3
Little Gem 14–15
parsley 114–15
rice noodle 18–19
Sicilian fennel 104–5
smoky aubergine 66–7
spring 150–1
squid, chickpea and chorizo
    96–7
stir fry noodle 156–7
tomato and mint 172–3
tortilla and bean 174–5
tricolore couscous 176–7
warm beetroot 68–9
warm chickpea 138–9
wild rice and feta 168–9
salmon
    and courgettes, chargrilled,
        warm salad of 100–1
    Thai kebabs, with sweet chilli
        and lime dip 92–3
salsa
    charred tomato 44–5
    mango 88–9
    Mexican 74–5
    tomato, cucumber and
        coriander 146–7
sandwiches, steak and
    caramelised onion 64–5

sardines
  with chickpeas, lemon and
    parsley 80–1
  with Sicilian fennel salad
    104–5
sauces
  BBQ 34–5
  fudge 184–5
  yogurt and tomato 124–5
sausages
  Cumberland hotdogs with
    charred tomato salsa 44–5
  sticky burgers with cheese
    10–11
sea bass with lemongrass and
  ginger, baked 110–11
shortcake swirl, fruity 202–3
skewers
  herbed chicken 42–3
  lemon and rosemary halloumi
    134–5
  oriental beef 54–5
smoothie jellies with ice cream
  190–1
spare ribs, sizzling 34–5
squid, chickpea and chorizo
  salad 96–7
steak
  and blue cheese wrap, hot
    52–3
  and caramelised onion
    sandwiches 64–5
  porcini-rubbed 72–3
  and roast vegetables with sun-
    dried tomato dressing 58–9
stir fry noodle salad 156–7
strawberry parfait 182–3

summer pudding, classic 204–5
sun-dried tomato dressing, steak
  and roast vegetables with
    58–9
sundaes, banana with fudge
  sauce 184–5
sweet potatoes, hot and spicy
  160–1
swordfish, seared, with mango
  salsa 88–9

tabbouleh, feta, with aubergines
  142–3
tapenade 126–7
tikka-style fish 86–7
toasts, spiced mackerel 82–3
tomatoes
  and butter bean salad 148–9
  and crisp prosciutto, pan-
    roasted chicken with 24–5
  cucumber and coriander salsa
    146–7
  and mint salad 172–3
  and potatoes, peppery, tuna
    with 84–5
  roast, with asparagus and
    black olives 154–5
  salsa, charred, Cumberland
    hotdogs with 44–5
  sun-dried dressing, steak and
    roast vegetables with 58–9
  and yogurt sauces, aubergine
    with 124–5
tortillas
  and bean salad 174–5
  cheesy wraps 128–9
  spiced tuna 98–9

tropical fizz, non-alcoholic 206–7
tuna
  with peppery tomatoes and
    potatoes 84–5
  seared, with parsley salad
    114–15
  spiced tortillas 98–9
  tangy burgers 106–7

veg burgers, cheesey 140–1
vegetables
  BBQ, with goat's cheese
    130–1
  grilled and marinated summer
    170–1
  roast 58–9
vin santo 182–3

watercress dressing 150–1
watermelon, mint and halloumi
  salad 116–17
wedges, cheesey garlic bread
  152–3
wine, red, refreshing cooler
  186–7
wraps
  cheesy tortilla 128–9
  hot steak and blue cheese
    52–3
  lime and pepper chicken 36–7
  roasted pepper and halloumi
    122–3

yogurt 46–7, 202–3
  and coriander dressing 136–7
  and tomato sauces 124–5

Picture and recipe credits

BBC *Good Food* magazine and BBC Books would like to thank the following people for providing photos. While every effort has been made to trace and acknowledge all photographers, we should like to apologize should there be any errors or omissions.

Marie-Louise Avery p185, p191; Iain Bagwell p69; Steve Baxter p27, p113; Peter Cassidy p121, p173; Jean Cazals p39, p43, p109, p131; Tim Evans-Cook p183; Ken Field p123; Will Heap p45, p47, p135; Dean Grennan p143; Lisa Linder p167; William Lingwood p65, p203; Gareth Morgans p6, p15, p23, p41, p51, p61, p63, p67, p89, p95, p99, p103, p107, p119, p133, p163, p177; David Munns p21, p35, p97, p105, p125, p137, p139, p161, p181, p189, p205, p209; Noel Murphy p171; Myles New p11, p19, p25, p37, p55, p59, p81, p115, p117, p127, p165, p169, p187, p207; Elisabeth Parsons p13, p49, p57, p83, p85, p87, p91, p147, p157; Craig Robertson p17, P93, p179, p211; Howard Shooter p77; Roger Stowell p31, p53, p149, p153, p195, p196; Simon Walton p101, p129, p141, p159; Cameron Watt p29; Philip Webb p73, p111, p145, p151, p193, p200; Simon Wheeler p71, p75, p79, p155; Tim Young p175; Elizabeth Zeschin p33

All the recipes in this book were created by the editorial team at *Good Food* and by regular contributors to the magazine.